The Ethics of Transracial Adoption

The Ethics of Transracial Adoption

Hawley Fogg-Davis

Cornell University Press

ITHACA AND LONDON

First published 2002 by Cornell University Press

Printed in the United States of America

Library of Congress Cataloging-in-Publication Data

Fogg-Davis, Hawley Grace, 1970–
    The ethics of transracial adoption / Hawley Fogg-Davis.
      p. cm.
    Includes bibliographical references and index.
    ISBN 0-8014-3898-5 (alk. paper)
    1. Interracial adoption—United States—Moral and ethical
aspects.   I. Title.
    HV875.64 .F64 2001
362.73'4'0973—dc21

                                  2001004391

Cornell University Press strives to use environmentally responsible suppliers and
materials to the fullest extent possible in the publishing of its books. Such materials
include vegetable-based, low-VOC inks and acid-free papers that are recycled, totally
chlorine-free, or partly composed of nonwood fibers. Books that bear the logo of
the FSC (Forest Stewardship Council) use paper taken from forests that have been
inspected and certified as meeting the highest standards for environmental and
social responsibility. For further information, visit our website at
www.cornellpress.cornell.edu.

Cloth printing   10 9 8 7 6 5 4 3 2 1

For my mother, Susan

Contents

Acknowledgments

It is truly a pleasure to recognize the many sources of inspiration, guidance, and constructive criticism that have brought this book into being. My sincere thanks to Mary (Molly) Lyndon Shanley for a rich, ongoing intellectual exchange about race, adoption, and political theory, and for encouragement. Janet Farell Smith read a later version of the manuscript and asked incisive questions. I also thank her for organizing in March 2000 the wonderful symposium "Ethics and Adoption" at the University of Massachusetts–Boston, where I presented my ideas about adoption and racial navigation and learned from a wide circle of adoption professionals and academics. Many thanks to Amy Gutmann, Stanley N. Katz, Robert Gooding-Williams, Tali Mendelberg, George Kateb, Jeremy Waldron, David Heyd, Sally Haslanger, Joan Hollinger, Larry Blum, Martha Minow, Randall Kennedy, Twila Perry, and Ruth-Arlene Howe for critical feedback and help along the way and to Catherine Rice for editorial guidance.

Research for this project was supported by the University Center for Human Values at Princeton University, the Social Science Research Council, the Mellon Foundation, and the Anna Julia Cooper Postdoctoral Fellowship at the University of Wisconsin–Madison. Some of my ideas about race-conscious adoptive placement were published in the *Boston University Public Interest Law Journal* in 1997. I am grateful to Henry Shue and Kathy Abrams at Cornell University's Program on Ethics and Public Life for inviting me to present my work on adoption during the 2000 Cornell Young Scholar Weekend. All the participants in the colloquium were exceedingly generous with their time and energy, posing tough questions in a supportive way. Iris Young, Molly Shanley, and Dorothy Roberts offered thoughtful and extensive comments. I presented the major strands of the book at the Feminism and Law Workshop at the University of Toronto in September 2000 and wish to thank all of the workshop participants, especially Jennifer Nedelsky and Joseph Carens, for a challenging and exhilarating discussion.

I owe a debt of gratitude to my dear friend and colleague Reuel Rogers for countless conversations about the relationship between personal and political meanings of race in the United States and beyond, and for good humor. Thanks to Dara Strolovitch for talking through these ideas with me and for her technical know-how. And to Catherine McKinley, thank you for being a fellow itinerant wanderer. Marion Smiley and David Leheny, my colleagues at the University of Wisconsin–Madison, took the time to read the manuscript and offered important insight and collegial support. Lynn Howie and Patrick Guarasci provided excellent research assistance in the final stretch.

The Ethics of Transracial Adoption

Introduction

In the mid-1980s, Mattel started manufacturing dolls that came with birth certificates and adoption papers. The new owners of these Cabbage Patch Kids, mostly young girls, could give the doll a new adoptive name and make the "adoption" official by filling in blanks on the adoption certificate. Marketing make-believe motherhood to girls is nothing new. But never before had adoptive motherhood been so explicitly marketed to girls. The U.S. public literally lined up to purchase this newfangled twist on the old theme of playing house. Cabbage Patch Kids were a phenomenal commercial success, outselling most other toys during the holiday shopping seasons of 1984 and 1985. The frenzy to acquire these dolls created the bizarre mayhem of future "adoptive grandmothers" fighting one another for any Cabbage Patch doll they could get their hands on.

Perhaps the popularity of these dolls signaled a breaking down of social prejudice toward adoption. And maybe the faddish appeal of "transracial adoptions" among American girls reflected eased anxiety over interracial family life in U.S. society. It was especially hip for white girls to "adopt" black dolls. Generic "ethnic" dolls were also coveted items. Hair color, eye color, and skin pigment that was fabricated to represent some of the physical differences found among human beings made each doll somewhat unique, as did "personal" trademarks like freckles, hair texture, and sartorial style. Since the 1980s, the variety of Cabbage Patch dolls has grown, and they continue to be a popular American toy. African-American newborn dolls are still top-sellers, often back-ordered on Internet toy sites. Mattel still makes generic "ethnic" dolls and has added "Hispanic" male and female dolls to its product list, as well as "The Cabbage Patch Kids Playtime Friend with Special Needs," which comes in "blonde," "brunette," or "ethnic." "Special needs" dolls appear to be young children and have two canes sewn into their cloth hands.

What does the commodification of make-believe human characteristics say about the adoption of real children who come from real families instead of cabbage patches? Can we separate fact from fantasy?

Real adoption is of course different from doll collecting. But there are at least two disturbing similarities between the two events. First, most adoptive children and their inanimate counterparts are treated as if their original families and racial histories should not affect their adoptive placement. Second, neither real nor make-believe adoption is sufficiently future-oriented. Cabbage Patch Kids stay kids forever, and the public debate about transracial adoption (TRA) proceeds as if the entire controversy were about infants who never develop the capacity to cope with the racial complexity of their lives as they mature. These blinders have resulted in truncated legal and ethical analyses of TRA that focus almost exclusively on the event of adoptive placement, ignoring or downplaying the broader racial context of a particular child's life.

This book aims to expand the scope of moral inquiry to include both children's personal pre-adoption histories and the futures of adopted individuals as they build their self-concepts in a race-conscious world. I develop a race-sensitive argument against invidious racial discrimination in adoption. Race should not be a barrier to TRA, but adoption policy and practice should be sensitive to the effects of a race-conscious society on individual children in need of adoption. Though many explicit forms of racism have receded since the 1960s, racial categories and their social meanings continue to shape Americans' public and private behavior. There is no getting around the fact that we live in a race-conscious society. Black Americans and others classified as being racially different from white Americans must recognize this racial imposition in order to make sense of how they are seen by others. This is not to say that people should accept their racial classification wholesale. Instead of passively absorbing third-person racial identification, individuals should challenge existing racial meanings by creating flexible racial self-understandings in a lifelong process of self-reflection and-revision—a process I call racial navigation.

Combined with a moral principle of nondiscrimination, race sensitivity establishes a theoretical basis for racially just adoption policy and practice. Transracial adoption illuminates a nexus between public and private racism—one that is often ignored by political and legal analyses. Private acts of racism are inextricably linked to public acts of racism, but U.S. law and politics have been reluctant to interfere in private race-based decisions, especially those concerning family structure. Adoption brings the private sphere of family decision-making into a more public venue, as prospective adopters are prompted to decide what "kind" of child they wish to adopt—a decision that arises only indirectly in traditional biological reproduction through the selection of a heterosexual partner. Private race-based decisions are made all the time in family matters, and these decisions shape public notions of socially acceptable family configuration. Such private racial aversion initiates a domino effect: Racially homogenous family structure affects housing patterns, which in turn affects the racial composition of public schools, all of which perpetuates de facto racial segregation in the social lives of most Americans. The public nature of adoption brings these private decisions, and their effects, into focus.

Although the term *TRA* generally describes adoptions involving adults and children of different racial classifications, the adoption of black children by white parents has defined the image of TRA in the public debate from the very beginning. This narrow popular image of TRA as a white–black phenomenon is striking given that adoptions of black children by white parents account for only a small percentage of TRAs and an even smaller percentage of all U.S. domestic adoptions. The first documented instance of white–black TRA occurred in Minnesota in 1948 and involved the adoption of a black child by his white foster parents.[1] It was not until the 1950s and 1960s that adoption agencies started to include black children in their services in any significant number. The height of white–black TRA occurred in the late 1960s, as both prospective white adopters and adoption agencies endorsed the idea of racial integration and the corresponding social ideal of colorblindness. But colorblindness was never implemented in adoption policy or practice, as the racial integration of adoptive families rarely included the adoption of white children by black adults, and most whites continued to request healthy white infants. Elizabeth Bartholet estimates that the number of white–black TRAs peaked at 2,574 in 1971.[2] In 1972, the National Association of Black Social Workers issued a public statement denouncing TRA as a form of racial and cultural genocide.[3] The number of TRAs dropped to 1,569 in 1972 and then to 1,091 in 1973 and then, according to Bartholet, to 831 in 1975.[4]

In 1975, the federal government stopped collecting national data on adoption. State substitute care systems have since provided the federal government with some adoption data on a voluntary basis.[5] Currently, the U.S. Department of Health and Human Services is compiling a national adoption database through a mandatory data collection system called the Adoption and Foster Care Analysis and Reporting System (AFCARS). Until this database is fully operational, scholars must estimate the racial breakdown of the adoption system. While there is some discrepancy among researchers, most surmise that the majority of adults seeking to adopt are white (about 67 percent) and that these individuals generally request healthy white infants, which are in short supply.[6] At the end of 1994, the most recent year for which AFCARS data are available, black children comprised an estimated 47 percent of the children in foster care, whereas white children accounted for only 14 percent of children in foster care.[7] These data are alarming given that, of the total U.S. population, blacks make up only 12.3 percent and whites constitute a majority of 75.1 percent.[8] Blacks adopt at higher rates than their white counterparts, controlling for socioeconomic class, but there are not enough black adopters to adopt all of the black children in need of placement.[9]

This distilled picture omits many variables affecting today's adoption system—such factors as the increasing number of private, lawyer-mediated adoptions[10]; international adoption;[11] surrogacy; and a veritable explosion in reproductive technology. These practices raise ethical and legal questions such as whether lawyers act as "baby brokers" in private adoptions, whether commercial surrogacy contracts exploit women, and whether human sperm and eggs should be transacted for in a free economic market. Like domestic TRA, these social practices involve race-based reproductive decisions that warrant ethical inquiry. The subject of this book, however, is limited to the descriptive and prescriptive uses of race in domestic adoption policy and practice. More specifically, I concentrate on the adoption of black children by whites.

That most prospective adopters are white and many children in need of adoption are black has been the case for quite some time. Although most white adopters choose to adopt white children, some are willing to adopt black children. As a consequence, TRA accounts for a tiny percentage of all formal domestic adoptions by nonrelatives.[12] Yet even though very few whites adopt black children, the public debate about whether whites should be allowed to adopt black children has been heated, sustained, and definitive. While the public "fire" over TRA has varied in intensity since the 1960s, when whites first began adopting black children in significant numbers, the issue continues to evoke strong, often visceral reactions from a great many Americans. Why does TRA rankle so many white and black Americans?

Transracial adoption symbolizes white–black miscegenation, a social and once legal taboo that has persisted in America since the slavery era. If Naomi Zack is right in her belief that the American family has historically been and continues to be "a publicly sanctioned private institution for breeding white people," then TRA undermines that institutional purpose in a deliberate and public way.[13] Transracial adoption raises vexing questions about race and the politics of the family—issues that lie at the heart of American culture. What is the moral and political value of race? How is racial classification related to racial self-identification? How should we conceptualize the family in law and public policy, as well as in popular culture? What are the limits of using law to combat racial discrimination? And is it possible to acknowledge racial categories without reinforcing the negative social meanings that have been attached to those categories?

These questions have far-reaching consequences for our personal and political conduct. Racial navigation, a metaphor for mediating the personal and political meaning of race, is theoretically prompted by TRA because a racial and genetic "gap" exists between parents and children. But racial navigation is intended to have application well beyond the confines of TRA. It is a practical compromise between the social-scientific treatment of race as a static variable in human behavior and political-theory arguments for justice that imagine colorblind utopias. In sum, racial navigation is both a coping device for living in a race-conscious society and a tool for eradicating racial barriers in family life and interpersonal behavior generally.

While social-scientific analyses of racial attitudes can lend strategically valuable empirical support to normative arguments for racial justice, they fail to capture the nuances of racial meanings in self-identification, interpersonal behavior, and family relationships. Quantitative studies of race tend to reinforce one-dimensional racial definitions that compress the multifaceted ways in which people experience race. Racial reductionism is often needed to translate individual and social conflicts into the categorical language of law and politics, but we need to broaden our vision of social justice to include extralegal, race-sensitive moral arguments as well.

Political theory, the humanistic cousin of political science, would seem a likely antidote for the racial reductionism of social science. Political theorists use the method of thought experiment to imagine political societies in their corrected form. Indeed, a virtue of political theory lies in its ambition to avoid becoming mired in political life as it is. Stepping back from the status quo can open up the psychological space necessary for conceiving political life as it should be. But political theorists often depart too radically from the practical constraints of current social conditions. It may be that a colorblind political society is morally optimal, but we have no experience of colorblindness and no road map to get there. Consider, for example, John Rawls's theory of justice, which asks us to imagine ourselves in an original position of equality, stripped of our particular social, political, and economic identities for the purpose of answering the question "What kind of basic political institutional structure would I agree to if I did not know what my particular social position was going to be?" According to Rawls, "Among the essential features of this situation is that no one knows his place in society, his class position or social status, nor does any one know his fortune in the distribution of natural assets and abilities, his intelligence, strength, and the like."[14] This veil of ignorance is to ensure "that no one is advantaged or disadvantaged in the choice of principles by the outcome of natural chance or the contingency of social circumstances."[15] In the United States, racial classification is an especially powerful determinant of social status. Rawls wants us to imagine that we might be any race. We might be black, white, Asian, or Indian. But can we really imagine ourselves as racially polymorphous?

Rawlsian mental gymnastics are neither possible nor necessary for imagining justice. We have no experience of being outside of racial categories. We are born into racial categories, and we cannot remove our racial self-concepts when we think about justice. Even when John Howard Griffin ingested drugs to darken his skin so that he could write about racism "as a black man," he remained a white man *playing* the part of a black man.[16] Arguably, there is some consciousness-raising benefit to such "play," but whenever one "plays" the other, one never *becomes* the other. And if one can never become the other in any experiential way, then Rawls's original position is likely to produce results that are based in promoting the interests of the self we pretend to cast off rather than the artificial self we pretend to put on. Tackling racism requires that we avoid pretense. Racial classification is an existential starting point, an involuntary association that affects, but need not overwhelm, a person's self-understanding.

Race remains central to our public discourse, even in the midst of widespread legal and personal claims to colorblindness. Think, for example, of President Bill Clinton's 1997 "National Conversation on Race" initiative, which entailed a presidential committee comprised of legal scholars and historians charged with examining the issue of racial division across the nation. In the spring of 2000, the *New York Times* ran a series of fourteen feature-length articles on "How Race Is Lived in America." And as we head into the twenty-first century, Internet users passionately debate race and racism with other anonymous Internet users across the country from the privacy of their living rooms.[17] W. E. B. Du Bois's prophecy that twentieth-century America would be plagued by the problem of the color line has been officially validated.[18] And there is every indication that our race problems will follow us deep into the next century.

Political theory's lack of attention to race is well documented by Charles Mills in *The Racial Contract*. Mills argues that political philosophers have ignored race in both their normative and descriptive theorizing—a "blind spot" similar to the myopia identified by Carol Pateman with respect to gender and the social contract.[19] Mills makes the methodological claim that "white supremacy" is a political system that "can illuminatingly be theorized as based on a 'contract' between whites [to exclude nonwhites], a Racial Contract."[20] In Mills's estimation, colorblindness in political theory has a two-pronged root: On one hand, there are very few nonwhite philosophers and even fewer African-American philosophers.[21] And on the other hand, "Those African American philosophers who do work in moral and political theory tend either to produce general work indistinguishable from that of their white peers or to focus on local issues (affirmative action, the black 'underclass') or historical figures (W. E. B. Du Bois, Alain Locke) in a way that does not aggressively engage the broader debate."[22] Mills's conception of "the broader debate" presumably would include the study of the relationship between race and various pillars of philosophical discourse, such as the idea of free will, distributive justice, and moral reasoning. At first glance, the present endeavor might seem a "local issue." My goal, however, is to contribute both to the crafting of public policy regarding adoption and to more general theoretical debates about the meaning of race and racial identity in contemporary U.S. society. These issues are relevant to key debates in contemporary political theory, such as multiculturalism, the relationship between theory and practice, and the role of "personal politics" in political theory.

Before previewing the arguments contained in each of the five chapters, I want to explain my decision to focus on the racial binary of white–black adoption. The racial demographics of the United States have changed considerably since the TRA debate began in the early 1970s. Although it is increasingly unpopular to proclaim the uniqueness of the white–black divide in what has been, and is more so becoming, a multiracial, multiethnic society, America's "racial obsession," the product of a long history of fraught relations between whites and blacks, continues to set the stage for how we think about the demographic changes we experience.[23] Steven Holmes, one of the journalists involved in the *Times*'s "How Race Is Lived in America" series, made this point when he said that all nonblack racial groups are politically and socially evaluated in comparison to African Americans. Holmes was responding in a public forum to a question about why the series focused so heavily on social relationships between whites and blacks.[24]

The tenacity of this white–black social divide is given vivid construction in the public debate about TRA, which has focused almost exclusively on whether or not whites should be permitted to adopt African-American children. I focus on this racial dichotomy not because I think it is good for U.S. race relations, but because I want to ground my normative theory of racial self-identification in the practical reality that Holmes flagged. I aim to address this binary directly as a way of proliferating a more equitable and just array of racial-identity options. A necessary first step in this direction is to sharpen our definition of race. We live with the presumption that we know what race is. We know it when we see it. But if asked to explain the basis on which we make this presumption, we are likely to be lost for words. We are likely, that is, to have difficulty coming up with an intellectually defensible explication of this everyday idea that has such profound consequences for how we live our lives and view the lives of others, for how we construct our families and view the construction of other families. Chapter 1 delves into the debate about the definition of race.

Biological explanations of the race concept have been thoroughly discredited, as have religious creationist explanations of racial difference. In their place, the notion that race is socially or culturally constructed, that it has no innate or essential meaning, has taken root in mainstream academic discourse. Postmodern theories proclaim the social construction of race. The work of Michel Foucault has been especially influential among political theorists in this respect. In Foucault's theory of power, categorical discourses shape and mold our self-conceptions, and are thus coercive.[25] Although Foucault applied his theory to the historically shifting binary distinctions between the sane and insane, the normal and deviant, many scholars have since applied Foucault's argument to categorical sexual and racial discourse. It is useful to become aware of the manifold ways in which racial identities are socially formed. And it is true that there is no such thing as racial essence. The problem with the social-construction view of race is that it tends to promote the facile logic that if the idea of race is socially constructed, then it can be socially dismantled in a blaze of colorblindness.

Why is the idea of colorblindness so alluring? The colorblind impulse holds considerable sway because the race concept is considered poisoned at its sociolinguistic root—namely, the conquest of the "new world" and the institution of African slavery. Following this logic, colorblindness becomes the righting of old wrongs. Old wrongs such as colonization, slavery, and the injustices suffered in slavery's aftermath must be righted, but this cannot be accomplished by ignoring race. The term *race* can be given new social and personal meaning. It is not doomed to negativity. The necessary corrective for centuries of racism is not colorblindness but a strong commitment to nondiscrimination as a moral principle that extends beyond equal-protection law into the realm of private racial choices.

I develop this broad-based principle of nondiscrimination in Chapters 2 and 3 by investigating the discursive divide between theories of colorblindness and what I term "racial solidity" in the public debate about TRA. Colorblindness is really an oxymoron. If "color" means anything at all, if it holds any social meaning in our lives, then we cannot help but see it. Those who invoke colorblindness usually intend for it to mean, "The government should not discriminate among citizens in the dispensation of basic rights on the basis of racial ascription." In this formulation, colorblindness becomes shorthand for negative liberty: freedom from state-sponsored racial discrimination. The Fourteenth Amendment, ratified in 1868, supports negative liberty: "Nor shall any State deprive any person of life, liberty, or property, without due process of law; nor deny to any person within its jurisdiction the equal protection of the laws."

Elizabeth Bartholet and Randall Kennedy, proponents of colorblind legal theory, lobbied for the current federal adoption law, which states that no federally funded adoption agency may use the race of the prospective adopter(s) or child as a factor in deciding placement.[26] This law repeals Section 553 of the 1994 Multiethnic Placement Act, which states that adoption agencies receiving federal funds can use race as *a factor* in deciding adoptive placements, as long as race is not the *sole* or *determining factor* in any placement decision.[27] Legal arguments against TRA have ranged from full-scale endorsement of only placing black children with black adoptive parents to moderated versions of race-matching. Twila Perry and James Bowen endorse the latter position, arguing that black children should only be placed in white adoptive homes after all attempts to place them with black adoptive parents have been exhausted. The argument that black children belong in black adoptive homes is based on a theory of racial self-identification that I call racial solidity. From the position of racial solidity, race-matching adoption policy and practice are constitutionally permissible forms of group preservation.

Although I disagree with the adoption policy advanced by racial solidity theorists, they are right to acknowledge and emphasize the importance of keeping race in mind as we deliberate about adoption policy. Attention to the concerns motivating racial solidity can open our eyes to the insidious effects of racism. We see, for example, that TRA does not occur in a vacuum, that the disproportionate number of black children in need of adoption indicates a web of racial disadvantage in American society: the fact that blacks are more likely to be poor than whites,[28] that poor blacks are more likely than poor whites to have their parental rights terminated by a court,[29] that white women who give birth to biracial babies may be motivated by racist social pressure to surrender their children for adoption. Transracial adoption helps individual children by placing them in permanent adoptive homes, but it does nothing to repair the web of racial injustice that makes so many black children available for adoption in the first place.

The picture of whites adopting black children symbolizes our colorblind aspirations, proof that racial barriers can be overcome by familial care. But colorblind ideals often fall apart in practice. Chapter 2 demonstrates how colorblind legalism fails to challenge private race-based aversion. Colorblind arguments in favor of TRA have focused selectively on the equal-protection rights of prospective adopters to adopt black children if they so choose. These arguments ignore the rights of black children not to be discriminated against on the basis of their racial ascription in the placement process. Colorblindness, a noncontroversial social ideal, is used to open up adoption possibilities for whites but fails to question the morality of choosing a child according to racial classification.

I do not want to force whites to adopt black children. But I do want to encourage all prospective adopters to think twice about the morality of choosing a child according to racial classification. Whites should adopt black children, and blacks should adopt white children. My support for TRA that flows in all racial directions is not founded on colorblindness. Instead, I propose a comprehensive moral principle of nondiscrimination that includes but is not limited to equal-protection law. Chapter 4 introduces a thought experiment to illustrate this broad-based application of nondiscrimination. The thought experiment asks the reader to imagine an adoption system comprised solely of public agencies. Private adoption has been eliminated, and the only way for people to adopt is through state-run agencies. Each adoption agency uses a policy of racial randomization to place children in adoptive homes. Prospective adopters are prevented from choosing children according to racial categories to safeguard the legal and moral rights of children not to be discriminated against based on their racial ascription. This hypothetical situation is designed to question the private race-based choices we make in family configuration in adoption and beyond.

The hypothetical elimination of racial preferences in adoptive placement does not mean that race is unimportant in family life. Recall that racial navigation means recognizing the existential and political salience of racial categories. Racial selectivity in adoption is suspended because most adopters exercise same-race bias in choosing children. If this sounds wrong, it is because the public discourse in favor of colorblind adoption law has painted a distorted picture of today's adoption system, leaving the misleading impression that a sizable number of whites actually want to adopt black children. The reality is that adoption is a last resort for most, and that very few whites want to adopt black children. Most whites prefer healthy white infants, and when they discover that such babies are in short supply they are more likely to adopt children of Colombian, Korean, and American Indian ancestry than to adopt African American children.[30] As one researcher points out, "The lack of demand for African American children is demonstrated by the fact that 'there is no independent market for black babies.'"[31]

Children of African heritage are more likely than children of other racial groups to be discriminated against in adoption—a fact illustrated by the choices that U.S. adopters, most of whom are white, make when they adopt internationally. According to Mark Courtney, "Korea, China, Romania, and several countries in Central and South America have recently provided the vast majority of foreign children for adoption by American parents. In contrast, out of 9,008 foreign adoptions by American parents in 1991, only 41 were of children from Africa [0.5 percent]."[32] Understanding the persistence of racial prejudice from the perspective of black children in need of adoption helps to balance the distorted perception that the only, or most critical, issue at stake in the TRA controversy is "reverse racism" against whites who wish to adopt black children. Whites truly committed to the ideal of colorblindness should be amenable to a system of racial randomization in which they are statistically likely to be matched with a black child.

Most of the objections to the thought experiment of racial randomization stem from biologism, the desire to make adoptive families look like traditional biological families. As I argue throughout the book, adoption is a unique social and legal practice that should reject biologism. Adoption is a more public event than traditional biological reproduction insofar as the state must coordinate the interests of three parties: the child, the original parents (usually only the mother), and the adopting parents. Children in need of adoption have life experience, no matter how short, that social workers must consider. The child's racial classification should not be a barrier to placement, but an assessment of whether prospective adopters are likely to facilitate racial navigation should be part of determining the best interests of a particular child. The state's involvement in the construction of adoptive families attenuates, but does not destroy, the constitutionally sanctioned privacy we expect in the formation of biological and informal adoptive families. None of this is to say that adoptive families are not "real families" or that once placement has occurred these families do not deserve the same privacy rights accorded to biological families.

Chapter 5 weaves together the two major theoretical threads of the book: racial randomization, a broad-based moral principle of nondiscrimination, and racial navigation, a theory of racial self-identification. While neither principle automatically triggers the other, the two concepts are compatible. Together, they produce a race-sensitive theoretical argument in favor of TRA and interracial family life in general. Transracial adoption highlights the practical need for racial navigation. In racially monolithic biological families, there is less likelihood that racial imposition will be questioned, since no racial anomalies exist in the family's racial continuity. The racial and genetic discrepancy created by TRA illuminates the value of recognizing racial categories as a first step toward challenging the static, and often negative, meanings attached to this system of racial pigeonholing. Families, both biological and adoptive, can and should be launching pads for initiating a lifelong process of flexible racial self-identification.

CHAPTER 1

Navigating Racial Meaning

An examination of the political morality of transracial adoption (TRA) must first inquire into the meaning of race. Few concepts have been so contested and yet, at the same time, so taken for granted. Almost everyone agrees that race is a salient feature of U.S. society. But there is tremendous disagreement when it comes to answering such questions as why race continues to be part of our sociopolitical lexicon, how race is socially and politically salient, and whether we should continue to use the term. Our public discourse thrives on the concept of race, but we seem to be in profound confusion over what exactly we mean when we invoke the word. Are we referring to something biological, or is race a socially constructed concept? What does *social construction* mean? Is race a consequence of some more determinant social process such as class, ethnicity, or nationality? Is it something we have or something we acquire? Which definition of race fuels the controversy over TRA? And which should we use in deciding how, if at all, race should figure into policies governing adoptive placement?

Two definitional spheres of race are relevant to the development of an adoption policy that is racially just. First, should race affect adoption public policy? If so, then how? Second, how should race figure into the self-identification of individuals affected by adoption and beyond? Racial navigation is a metaphor that attempts to combine the idea of identity flexibility and change over time with the strategic value of race-consciousness and sensitivity in curbing invidious racial discrimination. In Chapter 4 I introduce a thought experiment of racially randomized adoptive placement as a way of activating our moral intuitions about nondiscrimination. My hope is that policymakers will use both theoretical concepts to refine existing adoption policy and practice.

Racial navigation is not a precondition for racial randomization, but these concepts are consistent with each other. Together, they paint a more comprehensive picture of racial justice in adoption than many arguments in support of TRA. Racial navigation refers to the use of race as a personal source of identification, whereas racial randomization attends to the more public issues of adoption law and politics. A public–private bifurcation is a helpful heuristic device, but the distinction dissipates at the level of human behavior. Racial self-concepts affect public policies, and public policies guide people in their racial self-understanding. All public forms of racism implicate private acts of racism, and the same is true in reverse. This slippage between public and private is especially pronounced in the political debate about TRA, making it a useful case study for examining the connection between public and personal conceptions of race.

Racial navigation should begin in childhood and is a response to the imposition of racial categories. In a society where individuals identified by others as having a race are treated invidiously based on this racial imposition, some degree of race-consciousness will be necessary for making sense of one's environment. Although we may yearn for a colorblind society, or at least a society that treats racial classification as morally irrelevant, we should not dismiss the strategic value of equipping individuals with the capacity to navigate racial categories in the here and now. This practical recognition of race is especially important for children, because their immaturity renders them more vulnerable than adults to the absorption of racial stereotype. To move closer to a society free of invidious racial discrimination, we must first acknowledge the practical need for racial self-awareness. Which modes of racial self-identification promote racial justice, and which do not?

The first section of this chapter addresses this question by sketching the theoretical contours of racial navigation. I further develop the idea of racial navigation in the second and third sections through a critical examination of two incisive meditations on the race concept. The theoretical work of historical sociologist Orlando Patterson and that of philosopher K. Anthony Appiah has been instrumental in helping me to sharpen my own definition of the elusively present idea of race. The fourth and final section shows how both of these arguments contribute to the idea of racial navigation. Patterson ironically teaches us that a racial dichotomy between black and white is an entrenched feature of U.S. society. Appiah gives us a valuable mode of personal identity that avoids the trap of racial confinement but fails to bear directly on politics. Racial navigation acknowledges the persistence of a white–black sociopolitical paradigm and its continued effect on the political and social incorporation of nonblack racial and ethnic minorities such as American Indians, Asian Americans, and Latinos/Latinas.

RACIAL NAVIGATION

Race operates on two distinct but related conceptual levels in the United States. On one level, race is a structural variable that predates individuals. In this sense, *race* refers to a race-conscious social environment into which we are born. The term *structural variable* acknowledges the mutability of racial categories as social and political factors over time and from place to place, a sociopolitical process that Michael Omi and Howard Winant dub racial formation. While their theory of racial formation helps to describe our social environment, it does not adequately address subjective responses to racial structure.[1] Individuals respond to the weight of racial categories that shape their society in myriad ways. Responses to structural notions of race can and do affect existing racial meanings. Collective responses to racial categories, in the form of organized political pressure, have forced changes in the U.S. racial order, as in the case of legal and political victories won by the civil rights movement in the 1950s and 1960s. Both the civil rights movement in the South and subsequent social movements of Black Power in northern cities involved black Americans working with nonblack allies to challenge the morality and constitutionality of de jure racism. Antiracist political activism could not be detached from the personal racial self-concepts of its participants and spectators, as film footage of police brutality forced Americans to contemplate their own action or inaction in the face of Jim Crow laws. But critical self-reflection is not automatic, especially when it touches on difficult topics like racism and one's personal responsibility for racism's perpetuation.

Transracial adoption can be a catalyst for this personal introspection by drawing our attention to the thin line between public and private acts of racism. Black children adopted by white parents must navigate both being racially different from their parents and the absence of a genetic family tie to their parents. Mending these fissures is a lifelong project that is both public and personal. Racial navigation can and should be practiced by everyone, but it is more likely to be triggered when an individual confronts a descriptive gap between her own racial classification and that of her immediate social setting: the family. The personal testimonies of transracial adoptees, as well as biracial and multiracial people raised in biologically based families, provide some of the most compelling examples of racial navigation.[2]

These individuals must carve their own racial self-identifications out of existing racial frameworks. Racial categories comprising the decennial U.S. Census set the stage for such navigation. The mutability of U.S. racial structure is illustrated by the fact that the census categories have changed almost every ten years since the first census was conducted in 1790 under the supervision of Thomas Jefferson.[3] Demographic data gathered by each census affect everything from congressional apportionment to the enforcement of civil rights legislation and federal affirmative action programs. Census categories also affect personal conceptions of race: "By attempting to provide a way for Americans to describe themselves, the categories actually began to shape those identities."[4] The trend toward self-reporting began with the 1970 census. Previously, census workers were instructed to use their own judgment to racially classify individuals. In subsequent years, both the self-classification and the opinion of enumerators were sometimes included. The 2000 census marked a decisive turn toward self-reporting, as it asked people not only to racially identify themselves, but also invited them to check more than one racial designation. Although the multiple check option fell short of the multiracial category that some had pushed for, debate about the configuration of the 2000 census sparked a valuable public discussion about the relationship between personal and political racial identification that will hopefully continue.

Racial categories are subject to historical alteration and now to personal interpretation. But it is also true that "the one-drop rule," the social convention that anyone with "one drop" of "black blood" is black, continues to shape popular understanding (or misunderstanding) about race. This once official and now unofficial rule applies even to people who are *perceived* as having some black ancestry.[5] Individuals must respond to this social convention when they contemplate their own racial classification. We can make choices within and against these categories, but we cannot escape them. For instance, a person with one biological parent who self-identifies as Korean American and another parent who self-identifies as African American may define herself as biracial, multiracial, or "just a person." But she must still express her self-identification within the parameters of socially recognized racial categories. Even if she refuses to fill out her census form, she must live in a social world built on census categories. Others are likely to treat her as a black woman based on social convention. She might develop and express a strong biracial or multiracial *personal* self-identification, yet adopt a *public* understanding of herself as African American to avoid cognitive dissonance. She may also check the box for African American on a census form based on a feeling of racial solidarity with others similarly labeled. Feelings of racial solidarity based on what Michael Dawson, Katherine Tate, and others have termed linked fate, appears to be especially strong among those identified by others as African American.[6] While 37 percent of those who checked the Native American box on the 2000 census also checked another racial box, usually white, only five percent of those who checked African American/black also checked another racial category.[7]

Racial solidarity can be compatible with racial navigation as long as it does not slip into racial solidity. Racial solidity connotes a solid, inflexible notion of racial self-identification that is preferably, according to its proponents, set in early childhood. Advocates of racial solidity, such as black cultural nationalists, equate a specific set of cultural practices with a normative vision of racial identity that fails to distinguish between personal and public notions of race. This rigidity tends to promote intragroup policing rather than critical reflection about racial identity. The Black Students Association (BSA) at the college I attended launched a "public service" campaign in the early 1990s that walked a fine line between racial solidarity and racial solidity. Members of the BSA posted signs around campus that read, "Are you perpetuating a stereotype?" The question was aimed at black undergraduates, although I wonder what effect it had on other students and regular citizens who read it. The signs were deliberately unavoidable, and the question stuck with you. There were at least two ways of interpreting this campaign. On one hand, the signs reminded us to reflect on our own behavior, to ask ourselves if our behavior was confirming stereotypes in the minds of our white classmates. But on the other hand, the signs echoed another set of racial expectations that could be just as stifling. "Are you perpetuating a stereotype?" was also a regulation: Act within the norms endorsed by the BSA, a subset of the black students on campus. The regulatory effect of the BSA's poster campaign was mitigated by the sometimes illuminating, sometimes sophomoric debate it generated among black students. The campaign reminds me that racial solidarity can be consistent with racial navigation as long as a person recognizes her racial group identification as strategic, flexible, and not overwhelming.

The BSA poster campaign shows us that racial self-identification is better conceived as an active process than a resolved issue. Active response to racial categories should change over time and vary from person to person, as individuals personalize their racial self-concepts. Personalization of one's racial self-concept lends stability and coherence to the potentially nebulous idea of "myself" amidst a sea of social flux. This self is neither a colorblind self, which would deny the existence of race as a structural variable, nor a solid racial self-concept, which would deny our capacity and moral responsibility to critically respond to racial classification.

Racial categories establish existential starting points. These categories are socially constructed, not biologically determined. As Naomi Zack observes, "In logical, causal terms, there are no necessary, necessary and sufficient, or sufficient racial characteristics, or genes for such characteristics, which every member of a race has."[8] While the physical characteristics we associate with physical race "can be passed on during some event of conception, . . . it cannot be predicted which or even if any physical characteristic will be passed on during any one event of conception."[9] The social definition of race is based on physical characteristics that are traced back to a person's biological parents. When we encounter someone whom we cannot immediately place in one racial category, we often look to her parents for clues. This, of course, does not mean that a black person is biologically different from a white person. It means that racial categories cannot be easily dismantled.

As an integral part of our social ontology, racial categories will persist into the foreseeable future. My advocacy of racial self-awareness should not be misconstrued as a celebration of racial categories. The race concept has more often than not been used to rationalize a battery of injustice, from slavery to contemporary practices such as "racial profiling" used by police and department stores to increase surveillance and interrogation of blacks and Latinos and Latinas.[10] A person's perceived racial classification reveals nothing about her character. Race, as indicated by skin color, facial features, and hair texture, is therefore an extremely poor predictor of human compatibility in friendship, romance, or adoption. Ideally, the concept of race would carry no moral weight. Ideals can be critical levers for imagining social and political change, but not if they are "moral standards that no one ever meets or even approximates in their actual behavior."[11] How might we cope, and even flourish, in our present race-conscious situation? A self thus conceived is a problem-solver, a virtue underscored by Stephen Jay Gould when he rhetorically asks, "What is intelligence, if not the ability to face problems in an unprogrammed (or, as we often say, creative) manner?"[12]

We need to talk about race, exploring both its negative origins and positive possibilities, in order to understand what is at stake in the public debate about TRA. One pivotal issue is the definition of family. Families are a significant part of the social structure we are born into, and they are typically conceptualized as racially homogenous. There is a strong assumption that we get our racial identity, along with a slew of other physical, mental, and emotional features, from our parents. In this respect, families represent critical transfer points for racial meanings, as children learn to see their own racial self-identification as the natural product of a genetic family tie. The idea of flexible racial self-understanding, one that is responsive to racial categories, challenges the assumption that we ought to acquire a prepackaged racial identity from a family. Instead of getting race from a family, individuals should cultivate their own self-concepts through conversation with family members, biological and adoptive, as well as through less intimate dialogue with people outside of one's family.[13] Because emotional identification affects racial navigation, and our strongest emotional ties are usually to members of our immediate families, we should expect the most intense exchange of ideas about racial self-awareness to occur within immediate families. Identity conversation describes both what is said and not said because both public and private opinions affect racial navigation. As a matter of moral proximity, the intensity of racial navigation is likely to decrease as one moves beyond one's immediate family to extended kin, friends, acquaintances, and strangers.

This conversational (family) and dialogical (others) self-understanding must not ignore or minimize the extent to which personal license in identity construction is practically constrained by extant racial categories. Reconciling the freedom of self-fashioning with the everyday imposition of racial classification is not easy. I am sympathetic to both Orlando Patterson's and K. Anthony Appiah's efforts to interrupt a long history of pejorative deployments of the race concept. Primarily, they wish to deflate the misconception that race is biologically determined. In making this argument, however, both theorists underestimate our capacity and practical need to think about race in both our personal and public lives.

PATTERSON'S REJECTION OF RACE

The thesis advanced by Patterson in *The Ordeal of Integration* serves as an important foil for racial navigation. Patterson rejects the term *race*, citing its notorious past as a tool of domination. In its place he proposes that we speak of *ethnicity*. Thus we should no longer speak of blacks and whites but use the ethnic terms *Afro-American* and *Euro-American* instead. With this linguistic twist, Patterson aims to encourage a public debate about ethnic justice, asking us to abandon what he calls an impoverished public discourse over "racial justice": "I think the time has come to abandon the terms black and white in reference to Americans. They are linguistically loaded terms and emphasize the physical, which is precisely what we want to get away from in interethnic relations."[14]

Patterson's normative claim here rests on his larger argument against biological—or, more pointedly, genetic—determinism. The goal of exposing the racism driving pseudo-scientific projects like *The Bell Curve* is sound, but justice does not require us to stop talking about race altogether.[15] Although its social meaning has shifted over time, race has remained a prominent feature of American political life. We must therefore engage the social meaning of race directly if we hope to devise realistic solutions to current events of racial injustice. Otherwise, we risk missing the target of racism altogether. Patterson ironically proves this very point by merely giving new names to an old conceptual divide between black and white.

Patterson tries to revive an old sociological framework in the service of furthering a project of ethnic justice. To his credit, his ethnic analogy argument is not easily placed in either the "progressive" sociological camp of the 1920s and 1930s or the "neoconservative" camp of the present era. Yet in trying to avoid the pitfalls of these "schools," Patterson ironically ends up fortifying the very white–black binary he set out to dissolve. Race, according to the ethnicity model, is an epiphenomenal consequence of a larger process of ethnicization; it is not a phenomenon unto itself that should be studied apart from the overriding process of ethnicization. The impetus for Patterson's critique of current "race talk" can be traced back to the emergence of an ethnicity-based sociological paradigm in the 1920s and 1930s. Horace Kallen and Robert Park introduced the ethnicity-based theories of cultural pluralism and assimilation, respectively, to refute claims of biologically based racial inferiority that were being invoked by scientists and political leaders of the time to justify the "natural" racial order propped up by southern Jim Crow laws. Scientific racism also influenced the behavior of politicians and citizens in the North, but its appeal was not as explicit and widespread as in the South. For their attack on nineteenth-century racist science, the early ethnicity-based sociologists won the label "progressive."

There was something "progressive" about challenging the deeply entrenched European and American idea that race was biologically determined. In the early part of the nineteenth century, many European and American scientists claimed that people of different races were of different species.[16] The publication of Charles Darwin's *Origin of Species* in 1859 deflated this theory of permanent racial types "by showing that in nature species were not permanent entities but were subject to evolution by adaptation and selection."[17] This revolution ushered in what has become known as social Darwinism: the attempt to use Darwin's claims to explain, and in the case of eugenicists to manipulate, social relations and outcomes. Where their predecessors had spoken of racial types, social Darwinists spoke of populations. Still, the net result was the same: racism backed by the authority of science. Margaret Sanger's eugenic pronouncements that birth control should be made available to the public primarily to curb the reproduction of "genetically inferior races" exemplifies social Darwinism, as do persistent "culture of poverty" arguments that poor blacks and Latinos/Latinas exhibit cultural habits and values of arrested development.[18]

Against the backdrop of social-scientific inquiry into race relations, the Chicago School of the 1920s and 1930s emerged in sharp relief: "In contrast to biologically oriented approaches, the ethnicity paradigm was an insurgent theory which suggested that race was a social category."[19] But race was not a social category unto itself. Rather, the ethnicity theorists treated race as just one of many social factors shaping ethnic groups. Students of American pluralism in the 1950s and 1960s were confident that the political interests of these ethnic groups would overlap with the interests of other social groups in the national legislative process, thereby ensuring their political representation.[20] Critics of what E. E. Schattschneider sarcastically labeled "the pluralist heaven" have since argued that racial minorities are poorly represented in interest-group politics, and that the process often works to exacerbate racial inequalities within racial interest groups based on sex, class, and sexual orientation.[21] African Americans continue to be square pegs in U.S. models of political incorporation and cultural assimilation, and this is due in large part to their unique history in the United States. Unlike most Americans, black Americans who trace their ancestry to African slaves can claim no voluntary immigrant ancestry. And they are the only group to have suffered institutional slavery in the United States.

Patterson agrees. He acknowledges, and takes seriously, America's tortured history of racism. Indeed, he asserts that it is precisely because of this history that we still need affirmative action programs. Affirmative action "has been the single most important factor accounting for the rise of a significant Afro-American middle class."[22] And yet he insists that the way to remedy societal racism is to treat "Afro-Americans" as an ethnic group. He seeks to remedy a racial problem with an ethnic solution. But Patterson's ethnicity argument differs from black neoconservative ethnicity arguments found in the work of Thomas Sowell, for instance, because he acknowledges that racism is a lingering impediment to "Afro-American" social and political progress. Sowell argues that all significant racial barriers were removed by political and legal victories of the civil rights movement of the 1950s and 1960s.[23] To achieve political and economic success today, black Americans should follow the trail blazed by white ethnic groups like Irish Americans, Italian Americans, and Jewish Americans. He cites the relative success of black immigrants from the Caribbean to support the argument that race is no longer a significant barrier to black achievement. Sowell attributes lingering black economic and social marginalization to cultural deficits that are not shared by black West Indian immigrants.[24]

Michael Omi and Howard Winant point to ethnicity theory's awkward, one-dimensional version of black exceptionalism. They argue that "the notion of uniqueness' doesn't go far enough because it is still posed within the ethnic group framework, while 'black,' like 'white,' is a palpably racial category."[25] Omi and Winant's point is that black Americans, by definition, cannot be squeezed into a paradigm based in the concept of variegated white identity. As Mary Waters shows, most contemporary white Americans think of their ethnic identification as optional, whereas black Americans can never fully escape their racial classification.[26] But Patterson's argument is different from the kind of ethnicity theory that Omi and Winant are criticizing. He does not say that Afro-Americans are like Irish Americans, Italian Americans, or Jewish Americans. Rather, he explicitly states that Afro-Americans are like Euro-Americans. But what does the term *Euro-American* refer to, if not persons we typically think of, within a racial paradigm, as white? He contends that "if we abandon the term *black*, however—whether in favor of African American or Afro-American—it makes no sense to continue to use the term *white*. I will therefore use the term *Euro-Americans* to describe the people elsewhere known as *whites*."[27] What at first seemed like nothing more than a reissue of an old theory of ethnicity turns out, in the end, to revert back to the very binary Patterson had set out to challenge: white and black. Why does Patterson make such a specious claim?

Perhaps the answer is found in a set of commitments that are hard to reconcile. The people Patterson calls Afro-Americans continue to be denied full incorporation into American pluralism in various ways. And yet they continue to be an integral part of American identity. As Patterson notes, "Afro-Americans, as I have emphasized throughout these essays, are not a different tribe or people with exotic cultural practices. They are, to repeat, among the most American of Americans, with as much variation as exists among Euro-Americans. These variations, however, are well within the cultural compass of all ordinary Americans."[28] From these words one can divine arguments for both assimilation and cultural pluralism. Clearly Patterson is trying to steer us away from racial stereotyping that distorts both first- and third-person perceptions of identity. But challenging stereotypes does not require a wholesale repudiation of the idea of race. This is not to dismiss the political significance of renaming a social group, especially one that still suffers group-based oppression. Semantic shifts from *colored* to *Negro* to *black* to *Afro-American* and to *African American* with or without a hyphen reflect milestones in political and cultural battles. But these changes never called for a moratorium on "race talk." Instead, linguistic fluidity in the expression of group-based racial identity shows that racial justice in the United States has been and continues to be a work-in-progress.

George Kateb takes Patterson's rejection of race to a more extreme destination, arguing that "the whole practice of categorization" should be discredited because it necessarily renders impossible "thinking of oneself as a separate individual."[29] But why should this be the case? Is it not possible to simultaneously think of oneself as part of a racial group and as a "separate individual"? Neither Patterson nor Kateb provides any evidence that blackness and individuality cannot coexist in a person. They end up subscribing to the very stereotyping they criticize by assuming ipso facto that no self-identified black person is capable of individual thought or action, and that all such persons are injured by racial classification. This narrow formulation of individualism treats black people as passive victims of racial imposition. In contrast to a flat conception of race, individuals can and do exhibit complicated racial self-understandings against the onslaught of racial stereotypes. To be a navigator of one's racial self is to establish what Patricia Williams describes as the "distance between the self, and the drama of one's stereotype; the distance between the nice internal spirit that is no one but oneself, and this wild image of projected fear." "Negotiating that distance is an ethical project of creating a livable space between the poles of other people's imagination and the nice calm center of oneself where dignity resides."[30]

Finding and maintaining this distance requires vigilance. The racial demographics of the United States are changing. Whites are now a minority group in California, as they are in New Mexico, Hawaii, and the District of Columbia. Many social scientists predict similar trends in New York, Texas, and Florida.[31] And yet even as America becomes a more racially diverse society, the white–black racial binary continues to frame our public discourse about race. Black Americans are still at the center of the race debate, as we tend to view all other racial minority groups through this bifurcated lens.

After more than three hundred years of the race concept, it is easy to understand the racial fatigue that compels many to wish that race talk would just go away. Fatigue is expected, but it is not a justification for permanently abandoning the onerous task of critically responding to racial meanings.

APPIAH'S REJECTION OF RACE

Like Patterson, K. Anthony Appiah wants to interrupt the current debate about race in the United States. And like Patterson, he argues that racial classification lacks scientific coherence. Ultimately, there is only one race in Appiah's view: the human race. But his rejection of race is not abrupt. He distinguishes between race as an intellectual concept and race as it might figure into the formation of individual identities. In other words, Appiah separates race from racial self-identification. While there can be no scientifically defensible meaning attached to the term *race*, Appiah allows that some conception of race may play a useful, albeit temporary, part in the process of personal identity construction.

The first part of Appiah's essay "Race, Culture, Identity: Misunderstood Connections" delves into the meaning of race. Two views of racial meaning are offered. Appiah then proceeds to prove that race lacks coherent intellectual meaning on both measures. First, Appiah considers the ideational view of meaning, which signals a relationship between a word and an idea: "Understanding the idea of race involves grasping how people think about races: what they take to be the central truths about races; under what sorts of circumstances they will apply the idea of race; what consequences for action will flow from that application."[32] Appiah's second view of racial meaning is referential. From this angle, race is defined by identifying "the things to which it applies, the things we refer to when we speak of 'races.'"[33] The ideational and referential views are often connected because "in practice, at least, access to an idea of race is probably needed to find the referent."[34]

If we are to believe in the ideational meaning of race, we must establish a set of necessary conditions or criteria for its existence. Appiah suggests two possible conditions: (1) People with very different skin colors are of different races, and (2) your race is determined by the race of your parents. Yet when we look around us we notice that those classified as black have an extremely wide range of skin color, as with those classified as white. Additionally, we notice that some people's parents are of different races. Certainly, the practice of TRA disproves the second condition, as the racial classification of children differs from that of their adoptive parents.

The referential view, according to Appiah, is simply the "historical version of what the ideational theory permits us to do." Here Appiah sets out to debunk the referential theory of race by excavating a history of the things the word *race* has been used to describe. Not surprisingly, this digging unearths a long history of derogatory descriptions of those human beings categorized as black, yellow, and red, conjoined with a celebration of the "white race" as comparatively superior in, for example, the areas of moral and cognitive psychology.[35] And as both Appiah and Patterson point out, these "differences" have been most deleterious for nonwhites when those with political power have invoked the authority of science to bolster such claims.

Racial prejudice and scientific authority can easily become a mutually reinforcing system of thought. As Stephen Jay Gould reminds us, people often turn to science to confirm their social prejudices so that "these latent prejudices themselves, not fresh data, are the primary source of renewed attention."[36] These latent social prejudices make the activity of linking biology to racial identity, in any manner, a precarious endeavor that is vulnerable to racist manipulation. Gould's critique of biological determinism illuminates this problem. His major claim in *The Mismeasure of Man* is that cultural evolution proceeds faster than biological (Darwinian) evolution.[37] Consequently, the range of human behavior at a given time in history is always extremely diverse as compared with anatomical or genetic changes in the human species. Biological determinists make the mistake of taking "the current ranges in modern environments as an expression of direct genetic programming, rather than a limited display of much broader potential."[38] Human beings are flexible, or at least we have the potential to be so.

The line between acknowledging racial categories and endorsing the negative meanings that have been attached to such categories is fragile. This fragility is precisely why Appiah urges "moving beyond" racial categories altogether. Anyone who has experienced the weight of racial stereotype knows how difficult it can be to maintain personal space between the "drama" and oneself. Such personal struggle is portrayed in the short story "Drinking Coffee Elsewhere," by Z. Z. Packer. Dina, a young black woman from Baltimore, is not enjoying freshmen orientation games at Yale, one of which invites students to depersonify themselves into a favorite object:

> When it was my turn I said, "My name is Dina, and if I had to be any object, I guess I'd be a revolver." The sunlight dulled as if on cue. Clouds passed rapidly overhead, presaging rain. I don't know why I said it. Until that moment I'd been good in all the ways that were meant to matter. I was an honor-roll student—though I'd learned long ago not to mention it in the part of Baltimore where I lived. Suddenly I was hard-bitten and recalcitrant, the kind of kid who took pleasure in sticking pins into cats; the kind who chased down smart kids to spray them with mace.[39]

Racial imposition brings the specter of racial stereotype, and it is often difficult to see oneself apart from the racial expectations of others. In light of this anxiety, Appiah implores us to adopt what he calls a "banal postmodern" approach to personal identity: "Live with fractured identities; engage in identity play; find solidarity, yes, but recognize contingency, and, above all, practice irony."[40] This invitation is attractive, for it opens a wide variety of possibilities for thinking and rethinking one's self-concept.

Irony is one response to racial imposition. The "identity play" of being ironic presupposes the existence of recognized boundaries, such as the line between blackness and whiteness or the cordoning off of male from female. The audience must understand that a transgression has occurred. For example, when RuPaul, a black drag queen supermodel, sports a voluminous platinum blonde wig, stiletto heels, and haute-couture women's clothing, he is being ironic. We recognize that he is a black man performing a stereotypical hyperfemininity most often associated with white female fashion models. According to Judith Butler, "In this sense, then, drag is subversive to the extent that it reflects on the imitative structure by which hegemonic gender is itself produced and disputes heterosexuality's claim on naturalness and originality."[41] RuPaul's performance would not be ironic if he were successfully passing for a white woman. I don't suppose that Appiah's invitation to "identity play" beckons us all to follow in RuPaul's ample footsteps. But maybe on a more modest scale, ironic acts of racial subversion can help to expose the "unnaturalness" of racial categories—an exposure that can undermine the foundation of racism.

Another interpretation of irony, however, is that its playfulness cancels out its potential for seriously challenging politics. Postmodern play can be, and often is, dismissed as frivolous and self-indulgent. Irony can also be read as cementing categorical thinking insofar as the actor covers up one categorical identity by putting on another categorical identity that is equally, if not more, recognizable. bell hooks, for example, argues that the commercially successful independent film *Paris Is Burning* reinforces stereotypes of normative white femininity because so many of the black drag queens in the film try to emulate white supermodels.[42] In the end, the effect of playing with existing racial and gender categories may be more entertainment than politics.

Judy Scales-Trent's autobiographical essays in *Notes of a White Black Woman* pose a more direct challenge to the existing racial order. Scales-Trent contemplates her own sense of self amidst U.S. historical distress over race "mixing." Having grown up as a "colored" girl in North Carolina during segregation and then in New York City, she describes the paradox of belonging to a black family and being seen by others as white because of her light skin and "European" facial features. She writes, "Many in my family are various shades of brown, as is common in most black families. Many of us, however, look white."[43] The oxymoron "white black woman" demonstrates personal flexibility within the parameters of an ingrained social system of racial categories. Racial navigation is nonetheless hard work, as Scales-Trent attests: "This does not mean that there is not, will never be, confusion or pain at being a white black woman. What it does mean is that it does not control me. It is a dilemma I live within. I center myself in myself, in the ambiguity of myself, and move on with life."[44] This is creative coping in the face of racial imposition. For Scales-Trent, racial navigation means turning an external contradiction into something internally coherent. She can do this because first-person racial identity depends on more than visual evidence; it contains a cognitive dimension, too.[45] Her personal sense of blackness stands at a critical distance from the flatness of racial stereotypes that would confine her to the trope of "tragic mulatto"—a person helplessly confused about his or her racial identity and doomed to a life of racial limbo.

Appiah's appreciation of this cognitive dimension of blackness emerges in his nuanced discussion about the psychological value of black nationalism. He considers, and is sympathetic to, cultural black nationalism to the extent that such narratives attempt to "construct a series of positive black life scripts" to replace negative racial stereotypes. So even though races have no empirical basis, black racial self-identification can be a way to heal some of the wounds caused by racism.[46] Appiah does not, however, want us to become "stuck" in racial boxes. Race might figure provisionally into someone's personal identity,

> but I think we need to go on to the next necessary step, which is to ask whether the identities constructed in this way are the ones we can all be happy with in the longer run. What demanding respect for people *as blacks* or *as gays* requires is that there be some scripts that go with being an African-American or having same-sex desires. There will be proper ways of being black and gay: there will be expectations to be met; demands will be made. It is at this point that someone who takes autonomy seriously will want to ask whether we have not replaced one kind of tyranny with another.[47]

Appiah does not specify under what circumstances a recuperative racial self-identification is morally or politically permissible. What exactly is meant by "the longer run"? Is this temporal reference to an individual's lifetime or to a later societal era? Is Appiah saying that a mature personal identity will always be "beyond race," while an immature or provisional personal identity might include racial identity? Or is he speaking of a collective project of someday eliminating all linguistic references to race?

Though I agree with Appiah's efforts to multiply identity choices and avoid racial confinement, I think that the notion of race can play a more explicit and enduring part in the sort of fluid personal identity development he sketches. Where Appiah speaks of "banal postmodernism," I wish to speak of flexible racial self-concepts that have no time limit. I now turn to a fuller statement of this racial self, incorporating key lessons learned from both Patterson and Appiah.

NAVIGATING RACE IN ADOPTION

Racial navigation is a metaphor for self-fashioning under the constraint of race that both addresses the social meaningfulness of a white–black racial division in contemporary U.S. society and seeks to encourage the sort of creative self-fashioning recommended by Appiah. For another example of racial navigation in action, consider the following self-portrait:

> Now, as a grown man, I feel privileged to have come from two worlds. My view of the world is not merely that of a black man but that of a black man with something of a Jewish soul. I don't consider myself Jewish, but when I look at Holocaust photographs of Jewish women whose children have been wrenched from them by Nazi soldiers, the women look like my own mother and I think to myself, *There but for the grace of God goes my own mother—and by extension, myself.*[48]

Here journalist James McBride tries to bridge the racial gap between his African-American father and white Jewish-American mother. He describes himself as "a black man with something of a Jewish soul." Why does he not describe himself as a Jewish man with something of a black soul? The answer is located in the social meaning we assign to race. Identified by others as black, McBride must make sense of himself by understanding this external gaze. You don't choose your racial starting point; others choose it for you. In Jean-Paul Sartre's words, "Such is the origin of my concrete relations with the Other; they are wholly governed by my attitudes with respect to the object I am for the Other."[49] And yet this meaning of self outside of self is only the beginning for Sartre, a subject I take up in Chapter 5. Like McBride, we can and should respond to racial imposition in creative ways. Or, to repeat Gould's directive, our intelligence should spur us to be problem-solvers.

Not all responses to racial imposition contribute to racial navigation. The term refers to a limited range of racial response and is not meant to be a welcome mat for moral relativism. What, then, is excluded from the ethical project of racial navigation? Shelby Steele's brand of racial response, for one, falls beyond the normative radar of racial navigation. Steele urges that blacks to become "bargainers": "A bargainer says, *I already believe you are innocent (good, fair-minded) and have faith that you will prove it.*"[50] The "you" refers to whites generally. By "bargaining," which implies giving something in exchange for something of comparable value, Steele believes that individual blacks will be able to "join the larger society."[51] Although this sounds trite, it is not overtly wrong. What is troubling is that the underlying conception of black personhood is simplistic. Either one is a "social victim" manifesting an "unconscious gravitation toward [victimization and poverty]" or one is a successful bargainer who "joins the larger society."[52] Steele offers no vision of a multidimensional black self—one that might contain both personal and public elements of racial awareness. Nor does he say anything about the impact of racial prejudice on the revered bargainers because he believes that any residual racism is mostly facilitated by a victim mentality. Glenn Loury supports Steele's critique of victimization: "I have spoken of the difference between the 'enemy without'—racism—and the 'enemy within' the black community—those dysfunctional behaviors of young blacks that perpetuate poverty and dependency."[53] The only flexibility offered by Steele and Loury is the capacity to "join" the majority, which is a poor advertisement for individualism.

Racial navigation aims to make explicit the interplay between a race-conscious social structure and individual self-understanding. Subsequent chapters develop the idea of racial navigation further, showing how it might be used to refine existing policies in support of TRA. From my theoretical analysis of race thus far, we can conclude that racial categories should not be a barrier in adoption. Racial categories provide individuals with existential points of departure but do not capture individual moral character. Racial self-understanding should not be grounded in the passive acquisition of race from a family. Instead, racial navigation is a dynamic process that actively cultivates a personalized racial self-concept through familial conversation, as well as through critical dialogue with others. Complacency in the face of racial categories perpetuates the dangerous misperception that racial categories are natural and thus scientifically discrete.

This theoretical notion of racial navigation differs from the idea of colorblindness, which I discuss in the next chapter. Whereas colorblindness ignores race in grappling with questions of political morality, racial navigation insists that race is a necessary factor in reasoning about both personal identity and public policy. So the difference between colorblindness and racial navigation is not necessarily found in particular policy prescriptions. Rather, the key difference lies in the definition of race that we use to think through policy questions.

In a representative democracy like the United States, legislation and the reasoning behind it should reflect the values of citizens. We rely, often unconsciously, on laws and policies to bolster our everyday notions of race and family—two contentious issues that have long occupied center stage in the U.S. political arena. Transracial adoption sits at the nexus between private and public realms of racial meaning. How we define race speaks volumes about how we imagine the relationship between private and public forms of racism. What sort of messages about race, adoption, and family life do we want policymakers to translate into legislation, and how should adoption practitioners carry out these beliefs?

Subsequent chapters address these questions. The main goal of this first chapter has been to explicate the racial meaning that is consistent with an adoption thought experiment called racial randomization that I describe in Chapter 4. To build the idea of racial navigation, I have borrowed elements from both Orlando Patterson and K. Anthony Appiah. Racial navigation calls for personal and interpersonal vigilance. Regrettably, such vigilance is still needed, perhaps more so now that scientific racism rears its ugly head once more in public discussion about the so-called pathologies of the so-called underclass. Stephen Jay Gould wryly observes that "biological determinism is rising in popularity again, as it always does in times of political retrenchment. The cocktail party circuit has been buzzing with its usual profundity about innate aggression, sex roles, and the naked ape. Millions of people are now suspecting that their social prejudices are scientific facts after all."[54]

In this atmosphere it is imperative that we be careful about the meanings we attach to the term *race* in our scholarly projects, political deliberation, and everyday conduct. I have argued that race operates on two conceptually distinct but related levels in contemporary U.S. society. On the first level, race is part of a social structure that predates us. On the second level, race factors into our individual self-concepts as we endeavor to live and understand ourselves in a race-conscious environment.

CHAPTER 2

What's Wrong with Colorblindness?

Colorblindness is an ethical ideal. If ethics tries to answer the question "How should I live my life?" then colorblindness tells us that skin color should not determine how we live our lives or how we treat others. We may never attain ethical ideals, but we might become better people in the process of reaching for them. Striving for colorblindness, however, can undermine efforts to make our own and other people's lives go better. The goal of racial justice in adoption requires that we see and acknowledge the color of a person's skin and, more pointedly, what that skin color represents in contemporary U.S. society.

In its current legal and social use, colorblindness marks a path of least resistance—not a good sign when dealing with entrenched social problems like racism, sexism, homophobia, and other mechanisms of social exclusion. In bypassing the difficult and long-term work of fighting racism, colorblindness has too often been cast as a goal that can be mastered by mere linguistic commitment. It would be better for the project of racial justice if we recognized that colorblindness is a moral ideal that none of us is likely to meet in our lifetimes. Then we might see the difficult chore of antiracism for what it is—hard, unrelenting, and absolutely necessary.

Colorblind ideology fuels the most prominent pro-TRA arguments. On the one hand, colorblindness represents a legal principle of nondiscrimination that prohibits adoption agencies from using race-matching placement policies. On the other hand, colorblindness is an extralegal moral principle that is to guide our personal and interpersonal conduct apart from legal dictum. In both cases, colorblindness crumbles in practice. Laws aimed at making the legal event of adoption colorblind disintegrate as social workers try to determine the best interests of a particular child without taking race into account. And when prospective adopters select a child against a social background of pervasive racial stereotypes and normative same-race family structure, it is difficult to believe that their personal decision-making process can or should ignore race.

As argued in Chapter 1, self-identification should take race into account not in the form of passive absorption, but in the form of active and critical response over a lifetime. Racial navigation is a way of thinking about oneself that avoids deception or willful blindness to race-based socioeconomic inequalities and race-based stigma. Colorblindness describes a perfect society in which no moral value is attached to a person's skin color, where "skin" is meant to stand in for the physical markers of social race: hair color and texture, eye color and shape, the width and length of one's nose, the presence of freckles on the face, body shape, and so on. Seeing race is necessary for understanding the society that infuses the word *race* with social meaning.

If colorblindness looms as an elusive ideal, then antiracism is the rocky road we have to hike. Antiracist work should take place both in the "public" arena of law and politics and the "private" arena of family decision-making, and involves recognizing and dismantling hierarchies that we may benefit from, psychologically and materially. As Drucilla Cornell writes, "What is not noted cannot be changed; thus by recognizing that, like it or not, we are white and Anglo because we are inevitably shaped by how we are seen, we are ethically respecting the need to call attention to the hierarchies as a first step in calling for their change."[1] The word colorblind is misapplied in arguments for racial justice in adoption because it washes over the critical work of antiracism in both law and personal conduct.

The first part of this chapter situates the term colorblindness within the legal-constitutional framework of equal-protection jurisprudence. Like the proponents of many anti–affirmative action arguments, advocates of TRA often invoke the ostensible colorblindness of a free economic market as the most efficient way to satisfy the constitutional ban on state-sponsored racial discrimination. These colorblind legal arguments hinge on a bright line dividing public or state-sponsored racial discrimination from racial discrimination carried out by private actors. But this legal line is not as bright as it might appear. As noted in Chapter 1, the border between public and private forms of racism is porous. This is not to say that government should intervene in every instance of racism. Rather, this permeability signals the need for an approach to adoption policymaking that considers the equal-protection rights of both prospective adopters *and* children awaiting adoption.

Yet, adoption policies should be grounded in more than legal arguments. The fact that many social workers continue to use race as an extralegal factor in placement decisions even in the face of colorblind federal legislation reveals something more than defiance. Serious and compassionate consideration of the best interests of a child must pay attention to social realities of racial imposition.[2] Instead of colorblindness, we should develop a race-conscious moral principle of nondiscrimination to guide both public and private aspects of adoption. While the principle of nondiscrimination does not automatically trigger racial navigation, the two concepts compliment each other.

COLORBLIND CONSTITUTIONALISM

The idea of colorblindness has a long history in Fourteenth Amendment jurisprudence. The Fourteenth Amendment to the U.S. Constitution, ratified in 1868 in the wake of the Civil War, bars states from denying citizens the equal protection of the laws. Equal protection, like due process, specifies procedural equality. The Constitution makes no promises about egalitarianism, or equality of outcome. As Stanley Katz observes, "The Reconstruction amendments wrote individual equality into the Constitution, but judicial interpretation limited its scope."[3] There is no question that the Fourteenth Amendment was enacted to address the obvious and extreme legal and political disadvantages of newly freed black slaves. But eradicating the vestiges of slavery in social relations was a far more formidable task, and one that Fourteenth Amendment jurisprudence has never fully addressed. Since the first judicial constructions of the Fourteenth Amendment during the Reconstruction era, judges have interpreted the "state action" component of the equal-protection clause to cordon off legal or civil equality from social equality.

After the collapse of Reconstruction in 1877, many Americans turned to the rule of law for social stability and authority. Morton Horwitz remarks, "After the trauma of the American Civil War, amid heightening social conflict produced by immigration, urbanization, and industrialization, orthodox legal thinkers and judges sought ever more fervently to create an autonomous legal culture as part of their 'search for order'."[4] Judges were extolled as neutral referees, whose job it was to use scientific deductive reasoning to match cases with pre-existing legal categories, leaving public opinion and their personal philosophies at the courtroom door.[5] Justice Harlan's famous dissent in the 1896 Supreme Court case *Plessy v. Ferguson* typifies this era of classical legal thought:

> The white race deems itself to be the dominant race in this country. And so it is, in prestige, in achievements, in education, in wealth and in power. So I doubt not, it will continue to be for all time, if it remains true to its great heritage and holds fast to the principles of constitutional liberty. But in view of the Constitution, in the eye of the law, there is in this country no superior, dominant, ruling class of citizens. There is no caste here. Our Constitution is *colorblind*, and neither knows nor tolerates classes among citizens. In respect of civil rights, all citizens are equal before the law.[6]

Harlan's dissent is noteworthy for its double-edged thrust. He objects to the Court's decision to uphold Jim Crow laws that forced blacks to use "separate but equal" public facilities, arguing that such laws must not discriminate against citizens based on skin color. But at the same time he enthusiastically endorses a stark social inequality between "the white race" and blacks, going so far as to long for an everlasting white supremacy. According to Harlan, Homer Plessy, the plaintiff, had a constitutional right to sit wherever he desired in a Louisiana train car. But the white passengers on that train had a corresponding constitutional right to demonstrate their racial antipathy and white supremacy toward Plessy in their social behavior.

Justice Harlan's words in *The Civil Rights Cases* of 1883 further demonstrate this bracketing of social race-based inequality: "No government ever has brought, or ever can bring, its people into social intercourse against their wishes. Whether one person will permit or maintain social relations with another is a matter with which government has no concern."[7] Exempting social relations from legal scrutiny creates a void into which any number of social arrangements may fall. And fall they did. The constitutional principle of colorblindness has been stretched in opposite directions to both support and condemn racial discrimination.

The adjudicative line dividing public from private racial discrimination has turned on whether or not an act of racial discrimination constitutes "state action." Supreme Court doctrine indicates the instability of this demarcation. Judges have disagreed over what degree of state or state entity entanglement with a particular act of racial discrimination is needed to trigger equal-protection law. In the 1880 case *Ex Parte Virginia*, the Court ruled that excluding blacks from juries based on their racial classification constituted state action in violation of the Fourteenth Amendment. Yet three years later the same Court contracted the definition of state action in *The Civil Rights Cases*. There the Court held that federal congressional authority under the Fourteenth Amendment was limited to racial discrimination executed "under the color of state laws," and that therefore the Civil Rights Act of 1875, which prohibited racial discrimination in public accommodations by both individuals and corporations, was unconstitutional.[8]

The 1940s and 1950s marked a slow but steady turning point in Fourteenth Amendment jurisprudence, as the National Association for the Advancement of Colored People (NAACP) waged its successful litigation campaign against racial discrimination in areas that had previously been treated as private, such as racially restrictive housing covenants (*Shelley v. Kramer* 1948) and public accommodations (*Heart of Atlanta Motel v. United States* 1964). The Supreme Court under Chief Justice Earl Warren (1953–69) treated Fourteenth Amendment jurisprudence as an active process of redrawing the line between state action and private discrimination. Building on the legal realist tradition of bringing social values and subjectivity to bear on judicial decision-making, the Warren Court infused equal-protection law with the moral and social value of racial integration. The NAACP's litigation campaign transformed equal-protection law into a tool for expanding the scope of public or state-sponsored racial discrimination.

Still, alongside these judicial expansions of state action, the Court has maintained that certain areas of private racial discrimination are beyond the reach of the Fourteenth Amendment. Most notably, the Court has held that racially exclusive private clubs are constitutionally protected. In the 1972 case *Moose Lodge No. 107 v. Irvis*, the Supreme Court under Chief Justice Warren Burger ruled that a private club that denied service to blacks did not violate the equal-protection clause because while it had received a liquor license from the state of Pennsylvania, it remained a "private entity."[9] The distinction between private actor and state actor was spelled out further by Justice Anthony M.

Kennedy in the 1986 case *Edmonson v. Leesville Concrete Co.*: "With few exemptions, such as the provisions of the Thirteenth Amendment, constitutional guarantees of individual liberty and equal protection do not apply to the actions of private entities."[10] Citing a previous case, *Lugar v. Edmonson Oil Co.*,[11] Kennedy continued: "This fundamental limitation on the scope of constitutional guarantees 'preserves an area of individual freedom by limiting the reach of federal law' and 'avoids imposing on the State, its agencies or officials, responsibility for conduct for which they cannot fairly be blamed.'"[12] *Moose Lodge* has survived several challenges over the years, which have strengthened its central holding that private clubs may discriminate on the basis of race without violating the Fourteenth Amendment.

The *Lugar* standard underscores the central difficulty and danger of relying too heavily on constitutional remedies for addressing racism. State action too broadly construed would encompass almost every adoption intermediary, as public and private agencies as well as individual lawyers must be licensed by the state where they practice. Adoption facilitators or "baby brokers" mediate many independent adoptions and are currently unregulated by state law. Nevertheless, one could argue that states become entangled in all adoptions because judges, acting as state officials, must execute the transfer of parental rights to adoptive parents and legalize any changes in the adopted child's name. This broad construction of state action would afford no "area of individual freedom" in adoption. It would hold states responsible for individuals' race-based choices. And in doing so, it would saddle judges with the difficult, and perhaps impossible, task of parsing out invidious racial discriminations from constitutionally permissible benign racial preferences.

Although civil rights litigation has been a critical vehicle for bringing local events of racial discrimination to the national fore, colorblind constitutionalism has been a limited and often ineffective means of accomplishing widespread and enduring social change.[13] Twila Perry, a critic of colorblind legal approaches to adoption, argues that African Americans have long recognized the limits of colorblind constitutionalism: "Although Blacks historically have asserted the ideal of colorblindness as part of their civil rights struggle, in the narrative of most Black people, the ideal of colorblindness is just that—an ideal. It has never been reality. Instead, race is what pervades the history and narrative of Blacks, and the link between the individual and the group has often seemed inescapable."[14] Willful blindness to this descriptive reality turns the job of fighting racism into a futile exercise of swinging in the dark.

Colorblind defenders of TRA focus narrowly on the racial discrimination of public adoption agencies, ignoring the racial discrimination of adopters when their selection of a child is based on his or her racial classification. Elizabeth Bartholet and Randall Kennedy train their legal analysis on the "reverse discrimination" faced by whites when they are prevented or discouraged from adopting black children. These arguments fail to scrutinize the race-based decisions of prospective adopters in the placement process. By focusing exclusively on the action of public agencies Bartholet and Kennedy give only a partial account of racial discrimination in adoption. With the exception of Richard Banks, no one has argued in favor of safeguarding the equal-protection rights of children awaiting adoption to be chosen without state-sponsored racial discrimination. I discuss Banks's argument in Chapter 4, along with my thought experiment of racial randomization. Bartholet and Kennedy's narrow definition of colorblindness in the debate about TRA should be replaced by a comprehensive moral principle of nondiscrimination that refers, but is not limited, to equal-protection law.

Bartholet and Kennedy's equal-protection argument stops at the point where this principle of nondiscrimination interferes with the freedom of prospective adopters to choose a child according to race. Piecemeal antiracism efforts in adoption prioritize the consumerlike freedom of prospective adopters over the moral right of children to be adopted without racial bias. The "private" choices of prospective adopters are made within a race-conscious society that places a normative premium on same-race family structure. As Bartholet herself concedes, "Most black and white prospective parents are likely to continue to choose same-race children to the extent that such children are available."[15] Colorblind constitutionalism permtis this same race bias, and is thus an insufficient tool for imagining a comprehensive picture of racial justice in adoption, which involves both private and public racial decision-making.

A LIBERTARIAN DEFENSE OF TRA

Many defenders of TRA infuse their colorblind constitutional arguments with the political philosophy of libertarianism. Libertarians imagine liberal democratic society as a free marketplace in which individuals make a series of economic transactions with one another to further their own life projects. Government is conceived as a referee, charged with facilitating this economic game: It makes sure that people play by the rules and fulfill their contracts. Robert Nozick envisions a "night watchman" state whereby government is to prevent the corruption of free-market forces by external price-fixing measures such as racial preferences and quotas in school admissions, employment, and government contracting. Market efficiency, the unimpeded flow of supply and demand, is thought to produce morally just outcomes. Thus libertarian theories clash with liberal theories that favor government intervention to correct for social disadvantage based on morally arbitrary "accidents of birth" such as race, sex, sexual orientation, and socioeconomic class (insofar as children cannot be held responsible for their parents' poverty).[16]

Two strands of libertarianism surface in the TRA debate: a radical policy proposal by law and economics jurist Richard Posner and a mainstream litigation campaign launched by the Institute for Justice, a conservative public-interest law firm based in Washington, D.C. I address Posner's radical libertarian policy proposal first to demonstrate the outer limit, or logical conclusion, of applying free-market ideology to adoption. Then I examine the more mainstream form of libertarianism found in the Institute for Justice's push for colorblind adoption law.

A Law and Economics Approach to TRA

In a controversial 1978 law journal article, Richard Posner, currently a judge for the Seventh Circuit U.S. Court of Appeals, and his associate Elisabeth Landes argued that the shortage of healthy white infants available for adoption could be remedied by "pricing" these babies higher than nonwhite babies, for whom there is less demand. Posner and Landes maintained that a free economic baby market, responsive to race-based preferences, would further the best interests of black and other low-demand children because their lower "price" would encourage their adoption.[17] They based this economic prediction on the shaky premise that "people in fact calculate in family matters, whether implicitly or explicitly, in the same way they do when purchasing ordinary goods and services," a conclusion culled from "studies of marriage and procreation."[18]

Adoptive children should not be viewed as substitutes for biological children. We should view adoption as a unique social practice that brings its own joys and difficulties. There is no justification, empirical or theoretical, for using genetic relatedness as a predictor for successful adoptive family life. Enduring family bonds can and do form among genetic strangers. Rebecca Carroll, a biracial woman raised by white adoptive parents, frames the argument against geneticism or biologism as a matter of honesty: "For people who choose adoption, there must be an overriding awareness that, after all is said and done, all the happy endings in the world cannot change the *facts*: the fact of a woman giving away her child; the fact of a child being abandoned; the fact that people are parenting a child who is not theirs."[19] Although Carroll's transfer of the possessive pronoun "theirs" to the original parents is jarring in its implication of biological ownership, she rightly points out that adoptive parenting is not the same as biological parenting. People who decide to adopt should expect a different set of parenting issues based on the critical, albeit short, histories that predate all adoptions.

Landes and Posner ignore this difference. They use biologism as a way of assigning market value to children. But because biologism implies racial continuity, their proposal actually reinforces the racial selectivity of prospective adopters. Free-market forces produce outcomes that add economic value to the norm of racial segregation in family life. Racial prejudice morphs into rational economic action. Any attempt to block race-based choice through the market would decrease economic efficiency: "The demand for babies for adoption is weaker among blacks than among whites, while the supply of such babies is vastly greater; so the price of acquiring parental rights over black babies would be lower unless white couples considered black babies a close substitute for white ones, which most white couples probably would not, even if white demand for black babies were not artificially depressed by opposition within the black community."[20] Posner tries to finesse the morally repugnant and illegal idea of selling babies by claiming that the good being bought and sold is really parental rights, not human life.[21] This semantic shift is unconvincing because the concept of parental rights is too abstracted from the actual demand expressed by prospective adopters: a baby. Posner acknowledges this objection, but his response is evasive: "Fair enough, but some of us believe that this and most societies could use more, not less, commodification and a more complete diffusion of the market-oriented ethical values that it promotes."[22]

Landes and Posner nonetheless draw our attention to the hypocrisy of current adoption policy and practice. Currently, children are effectively assigned economic value according to their racial classification in a number of ways. Many adoption agencies have variegated fee schedules based on the racial classification of children. For example, one U.S. adoption agency published the following fee schedule for adopting a U.S.-born child in 1990: "'white' infants . . . $7,500; 'biracial' infants . . . $3,800; 'black' infants . . . $2,200.90."[23] The distance between this policy and Landes and Posner's baby market is short and mostly nominal. Federal law in the form of the 1997 Adoption and Safe Families Act establishes bilevel monetary incentives to encourage state agencies to find adoptive homes for children in their custody. The federal government gives states $4,000 for each foster care child that it places in a permanent home. For each "special needs" child that a state transfers from foster care to an adoptive home, the federal government ups the ante to $6,000. Nonwhite children are often included in the category of "special needs," a designation that includes children with physical and developmental disabilities. The federal government should encourage adoption, but it should not stamp healthy nonwhite children with the label "special needs" and attach a higher monetary incentive for their adoption.

President Clinton's "Adoption 2002" plan provides direct economic incentive to prospective adopters in the form of tax rebates with the goal of increasing the number of adoptions nationwide by 2002. Financial subsidies to families who adopt children with expensive health care needs due to physical and developmental disability are certainly warranted. But we should be careful to distinguish these situations from the adoption of healthy children who are "hard to place" solely because of their racial ascription. Financial incentives in these cases convey the message that the adoption of black children entails a hardship that merits financial compensation. While today's adoption system is far from the full-blown economic baby market proposed by Landes and Posner, consumerlike values seep into current adoption policies and practice. We should stem the tide of capitalism in adoption, for it exacerbates the racial stigmatization of children.

A Litigation Campaign
Colorblind defenses of TRA can and do produce conservative social outcomes because they fail to investigate subtle and insidious forms

of racism that linger after formal or legal race-neutrality has been accomplished. The libertarian efforts of the Institute for Justice, a public-interest law firm led by Clint Bolick, exemplify this blindness. In language resonant of comic-book superheroes and the Hall of Justice, its Web site announces, "If you seek a courtroom champion for individual liberty, free market solutions, and limited government, look only as far as the Institute for Justice. When politicians pass sweepingly intrusive laws and bureaucrats build their empires of paperwork and power, only the Institute for Justice brings them to account in court."[24] In 1995, the institute launched a nationwide litigation campaign to "establish as a rule of law that racial discrimination in adoption is unconstitutional."[25] Elizabeth Bartholet, Randall Kennedy, and Laurence Tribe joined forces with Clint Bolick, an outspoken opponent of all "racial-preference programs," including and most emphatically race-based affirmative action programs. (Recall Bolick's 1993 op-ed piece in the *Wall Street Journal* branding Assistant Attorney for Civil Rights nominee Lani Guinier a "quota queen."[26])

The timing of the institute's widely publicized litigation campaign was deliberate. In the late 1980s and early 1990s, the subject of TRA reemerged as a hot topic on the public airwaves. Major newspapers and magazines, including the *New York Times*, ran articles featuring black and biracial young adults who had been adopted in the late 1960s by white parents. These families were presented as a post–civil rights movement experiment in racial integration, and the American public was curious about the results.[27] The talk show circuit, too, buzzed with the provocative issue of TRA. Even the silver screen shone for a moment on the subject, as Seth Margolis's 1993 novel, *Losing Isaiah*, was made into a mediocre Hollywood movie starring Jessica Lange and Halle Barry. *Losing Isaiah* recounts a custody battle between a recovering crack-addicted young black mother who abandons her infant and a middle-class white couple who adopts the child after he is rescued from a garbage dumpster. The poster advertising *Losing Isaiah* cut to the chase with a point-blank question: "Who decides what makes a Mother?"

In agency-mediated adoptions social workers decide. *How* they decide is the controversial question. Should social workers be permitted to use the race of prospective adopters as a proxy for good parenting? Is race-based evaluation of potential adoptive parents constitutional? When social workers use race in any part of their assessment of the best interests of individual children, do they engage in reverse racism? During the late 1980s and 1990s, public debate swirled around the issue of reverse racism, as whites sued employers and schools alleging that affirmative action programs had violated their equal-protection rights. In this charged atmosphere, race-matching adoption policies came under similar fire from both the political Left and Right. Senator Howard Metzenbaum, a Democrat from Ohio, introduced a "colorblind" bill into Congress aimed at ending reverse racism in federally funded adoption and foster care agencies. The bill was signed into law in 1994 as the Multiethnic Placement Act (MEPA).

But a long and impassioned legislative debate had narrowed the scope of the original bill. Powerful interest groups such as the Children's Defense Fund, the North American Council on Adoptable Children, and Adoptive Families of America opposed removing all consideration of race from the placement process. In the end, the bill's original language was changed to allow the use of race as a factor in adoptive placements, as long as race did not become the determining or sole factor in any particular adoption.[28] When does consideration of race become the determining or sole factor in a placement decision? This ambiguity meant that many agencies continued to use race as part of their placement assessments.

The year is 1995: Enter the Institute for Justice. The institute's plan was to establish, as a rule of law, that MEPA's allowance of racial consideration in adoption violated the Fourteenth Amendment rights of both potential adopters and children awaiting adoption. The institute argued that an agency's evaluation of prospective adopters should be colorblind. Its first and most important success was a 1995 case involving allegations that the Texas Department of Protective and Regulatory Services (DPRS) had discriminated against prospective adopters based on their racial classification. Lou Ann and Scott Mullen, a American Indian woman and white man, married and living in Lexington, Texas, became the foster parents of a black boy, Matthew O., nine days after he was born suffering from syphilis and with cocaine in his system. A month later, the Mullens attempted to adopt Matthew, but according to Ms. Mullen, they were told by the social worker handling their case, "Don't even think about it. He's a baby; he's black; he's going into a black home."[29] Ms. Mullen says that she requested to adopt Matthew at least five times and was rebuffed by the DPRS each time.

The DPRS removed Matthew from the Mullens' home on August 13, 1994, to place him and his older brother, Joseph, with a black adoptive family. The adoption was not successful. At that time, the Mullens inquired about adopting both Matthew and Joseph, but the DPRS told them that it was going to search for a black home for the boys. A black home would, in the words of the DPRS case worker, be in the "best interests" of the boys and "their culture." A 1993 Texas law barred public adoption agencies from delaying or denying an adoption "or otherwise discriminat[ing] on the basis of race or ethnicity of a child or prospective parents."[30] The DPRS interpreted this statute to allow for race to be used as a factor in assessing the best interests of a child in its custody, as long as race was not the sole or determining factor in any particular placement.

Texas's law mirrored the language of MEPA. Lawyers for the institute argued that allowing race to play any part in adoption was the thin edge of the wedge that would give social workers the power to discriminate against potential parents—both white and, in the case of Lou Ann Mullen, nonblack.[31] The institute filed a lawsuit on the behalf of Mathew and Joseph and a proposed class of similarly situated children. Under the threat of lawsuit, the DPRS changed course, informing the Mullens that they could now adopt Matthew and Joseph. And on August 18, 1995, the state of Texas finalized the adoption of Matthew and Joseph by the Mullens. The petition for a class-action suit was denied by the Texas district court. In November 1996, the parties to the case conditionally agreed on a settlement involving two parts. First, documentation of state adoptive placements would be turned over to the Institute for Justice, and state adoption agencies in Texas agreed to be monitored by the institute for two years. Second, "[the] DPRS was required to make diligent efforts to speed up the adoptive placement of two other African-American foster children who have lived with the Mullens for over five years."[32]

The institute's brief in *Matthew O.* cites the authority of Supreme Court precedent to show that "the Fourteenth Amendment's central mandate is 'racial neutrality in government decision-making.'" Moreover, "'Racial and ethnic distinctions of any sort are inherently suspect and call for the most exacting judicial examination.'"[33] A state-supported racial classification must bear a "compelling" relationship to a legitimate government purpose in order for it to be consistent with the Fourteenth Amendment. In a separate article, Randall

Kennedy comments, "This aversion to racial criteria stems from our long and bitter history with them, an experience that includes slavery, open, invidious racial distinctions, and *de jure* segregation. This history suggests that more often than not, there exists no good reason to draw racial distinctions."[34] Hence "race-conscious action has generally been allowed only where it can be justified on the grounds of compelling necessity, or where it is designed to benefit racial minority groups either by avoiding or preventing discrimination or by remedying its effects, as in the case of affirmative action."[35] According to the institute's brief, "[the] DPRS' race-matching cannot be defended as a remedial measure."[36] Nor did the DPRS claim that its policies were intended as a form of race-based affirmative action.[37]

MEPA AND NONCOMPLIANCE

The failure of MEPA to affect adoption practice in Texas and other states demonstrates a tension between the law on books and law in action. In 1996, MEPA was amended in an effort to narrow the gap between colorblindness as legal theory and colorblindness as administrative practice. MEPA II categorically barred federally funded adoption agencies from using racial classification in any placement decision. Not only did MEPA II eliminate the ambiguous racial language of MEPA I, but it also mandated stiff financial penalties for noncompliant federally funded agencies that increased with each subsequent violation. Private citizens were granted the right to sue agencies for enforcement of the federal law in court, as well as the right to have their lawyers' fees paid by the charged agency.[38]

Elizabeth Bartholet believes that no leeway should be given to agencies to consider race. In Bartholet's view, MEPA II should have repealed the provision in MEPA I that allowed agencies to make race-based recruitment efforts to increase the number of black and other nonwhite adopters. In her most recent book, *Nobody's Children*, Bartholet criticizes "creative" methods used by social workers to violate the spirit of MEPA II while obeying its letter. Bartholet argues that many social workers continue to take race into account under the ruse of "cultural competence" tests that are used to prevent TRA based on the assumption that whites lack the cultural competence to parent black children. Even the promotion of kinship care—the effort to keep children within their families of origin when their original parents' rights have been temporarily or permanently severed, and attempts to keep children in foster homes that are in or near their original neighborhoods—are deemed nefarious episodes of race-matching. For Bartholet, any consideration of race by adoption agencies amounts to race-matching, and all race-matching is racist.[39]

But there is another interpretation of these events. The persistent use of racial consideration by social workers may tell us that colorblind social work is practically impossible and undesirable in a race-conscious society. Racial animus will always cloud the judgments of some social workers. But Bartholet's accusation is more far-reaching. She believes that racism in the guise of race-matching constitutes a professional norm among social workers. "Soon after MEPA II's passage, newsletters from various child welfare organizations promoted creative 'interpretations' of its provisions. . . . In leading child welfare journals articles appeared with titles such as, 'Achieving Same-Race Placements for African-American Children,' telling readers how to accomplish race matching despite MEPA."[40]

But not all "creative interpretations" of colorblind laws are racist. How can a social worker evaluate the best interests of a black child without considering the social meaning of race for that child? Good social work involves attention to social context. Social workers have a professional duty to gauge how a specific social setting might affect a child in need of adoption in light of that child's racial ascription and other social identifications such as physical and developmental ability, sex, ethnicity, age, and perhaps religious affiliation. Children socially identified as nonwhite live under the pressure of racial imposition before, during, and after the moment of adoptive placement. Social workers should find these children homes that are likely to encourage racial navigation, the race-conscious activity of resisting the flatness of racial stereotype. Whites can and should encourage racial navigation in both their own lives and the children they parent. Correspondingly, black parents and parents of other racial ascriptions should practice and promote racial navigation in their families.

Racial navigation is neither colorblind nor a form of invidious racial discrimination. Bartholet's critique of race-sensitive social work ignores this distinction. She insists that colorblind adoption law should produce colorblind adoption practice: "The intent to remove race as a factor in placement decisions could hardly have been made more clear."[41] But if MEPA II was modeled after other civil rights statutes, as Bartholet says it was, then the purpose of MEPA is more accurately described as an effort to eradicate *invidious* racial discrimination than a general ban on every kind of racial consideration in adoption. Weeding out invidious from benign racial discrimination can be a difficult if not impossible chore, especially when adjudication focuses on the discriminator's mindset. Equal protection doctrine has shifted from focusing on the consequences of racial discrimination to examining the motivation of the discriminator. Did the predominately white, upper-middle-class Village of Arlington Heights, a Chicago suburb, *intend* to discriminate against blacks when it opposed the construction of a housing project for lower- and moderate-income families?[42] Did an employer *consciously* treat a black woman invidiously when firing her because her braided hairstyle violated a company policy against "unorthodox" hairstyles?[43] Kimberle Crenshaw dubs the past civil rights era a time of "racial retrenchment," as courts abandon former efforts to secure racially just outcomes.[44]

Even when the Supreme Court has addressed racially unjust social outcomes, it has been ill equipped to deal with subtle forms of racism that occur in mostly private associations like the family. Even legislatures, with their fingers on the purse strings, are limited in their ability to effectuate social change, especially in the realm of family structure. Formal rules for adoption practice were laid down by MEPA II. But that formal colorblindness did not mean that adoption practice had to ignore race altogether. The purpose of MEPA II was to remove invidious racial discrimination from federally funded adoption agencies, thus creating equal access to adoption.

Proof that MEPA II was not intended to be implemented in a completely colorblind manner is found in a set of administration guidelines issued in May 1998 by the Department of Health and Human Services (HHS), the federal agency charged with administrating MEPA II. The department defines good social work practice as "the individualized assessment of a prospective parent's ability to serve as a foster or adoptive parent."[45] This emphasis on individualized assessment does not lend itself to the kind of generalized colorblindness that the Institute for Justice advocates. Instead, HHS allows that race is a legitimate consideration in evaluating the "total needs" of a child and the ability of a prospective parent to "meet the child's needs." Here HHS draws a fine but important line between routinely using race as a matter of general policy and the use of race as a factor in particular placements. Responding to the question of whether or not cultural competency tests violate MEPA, HHS refers again to the difference between general policy and a case-by-case approach. They rightly reject the proposition that culture is a proxy for race, and so condemn the explicit use of "cultural competency" in placement decisions.

Joan Hollinger elucidates the fine line between race-consciousness and racial stereotyping in her *Guide to the Multiethnic Placement Act*: "Even when the facts of the particular case allow some consideration related to race, color, or national origin, this consideration should not predominate. Among other needs to be considered and typically to be given the most weight are: the child's age, ties to siblings and other relatives, health or physical condition, educational, cognitive, and psychological needs, and cultural needs, including religious, linguistic, dietary, musical, or athletic needs. In addition, the child may have personal preferences that he or she can articulate and discuss." MEPA II requires that racial consideration avoid stereotypical thinking, and that social workers document their use of race in specific placement decisions.[46]

One can read HHS's guidelines as confusing double-speak, or as attending to the nuances of performing good social work in a race-conscious society. Bartholet and the Institute for Justice take the former view. As proponents of strict colorblindness, they worry that any attention to race in the placement process will lead to reverse racism against whites wishing to adopt black children. I am not so naive as to think that race-conscious social work will never erect racial barriers in adoption. But neither am I so pessimistic as to believe that this will always, or even mostly, be the case. We need to give social workers the benefit of the doubt when it comes to assessing individual cases. Good social work should not prevent whites from adopting black children as a general rule, and HHS is very clear about that. But good social work does require an evaluation of a child's best interests within, not apart from, his or her social circumstances.

The advocates of colorblind adoption seek a guarantee that is practically impossible and normatively undesirable. As noted at the beginning of this chapter, we ought to put the ethical ideal of colorblindness in its proper place. Sometimes there is value in reaching for ethical ideals, and sometimes the very act of reaching is self-defeating—as, for example, when we fail to acknowledge the weight of existing racial hierarchy and our place on that ladder. If we define colorblindness as the idea that a person's racial classification should have no bearing on his moral worth, then colorblindness is certainly a worthy aspiration for interpersonal behavior. Colorblindness so defined is rightly aimed at fighting invidious racial discrimination. It involves critical self-reflection and self-sacrifice. Antiracism is a precondition for moving toward a colorblind ideal. Constitutional colorblindness concentrates solely on formal race-neutrality, passing no judgment on the private racial views held by prospective adopters. This is not to presume that all white prospective adopters are racist. My point is simply that these potential parents, like everyone, should reflect on the meaning of same-race and interracial adoptive family life. Social workers can and should help to facilitate this process. Indeed, they have a professional obligation to determine which homes are most likely to promote and sustain the process of racial navigation that I outlined in Chapter 1.

Too often the trope of colorblindness is deployed in the TRA debate and in our everyday speech as a defensive mantra that shuts down critical thinking about the racial classification of oneself and others. It is impossible to anticipate all of the ways that TRA will alter one's existence as a white woman or man. White adoptive mothers have written eloquently, often mixing academic arguments with personal and fictional prose, about how TRA has changed their lives as others begin to see them, and they start to see themselves as white mothers of non-white children.[47] These narratives illustrate racial navigation, as black children and their white parents must make sense of the racial and genetic fissure in their families. The law cannot, nor should it try to, *force* people to practice racial navigation. Law cannot force social workers to always consider race in precisely the right measure. Law can establish a formal set of rules that demarcate general parameters for social behavior. But the devil is always in the details, and that is where the tough, and necessarily subjective, work of race-sensitive adoption falls. We need a moral principle of nondiscrimination that works within and exceeds antidiscrimination law. Ultimately, we have to do the hard work of consciously fighting racism, both in what we do and how we do it, across the spectrum of our social conduct.

CHAPTER 3

What's Wrong with Racial Solidity?

In 1971, the National Association of Black Social Workers (NABSW) issued a public statement denouncing the practice of whites adopting black children as a form of genocide.[1] In 1985, William Merritt, president of the NABSW, more explicitly condemned TRA as "a blatant form of race and cultural genocide" in testimony before a Senate committee.[2] Black children, the NABSW asserted, should only be placed with black adoptive parents. While the impact of the NABSW's statement on the incidence of TRA is a contested matter, there is no question that the NABSW's harsh indictment sparked a public debate about TRA that continues today. In 1994, the NABSW moderated its opposition to TRA, allowing that when black families cannot be found for black children they should be placed transracially rather than in foster care.[3] This moderated anti-TRA stance shapes many of the scholarly arguments against TRA.[4]

Race-conscious objections to TRA have been a double-edged sword in the fight for a broad-based conception of racial justice in adoption. To their credit, scholars such as James Bowen, Ruth-Arlene Howe, and Twila Perry expose the inadequacy of colorblindness as a theoretical justification for permitting and encouraging whites to adopt black children. They make the mistake, however, of using this important critique to reject the practice of TRA, or at least treat TRA as less preferable than same-race placement. Shifting the emphasis away from colorblind deployments of equal-protection law to the more individualistic "best interests of the child" legal standard, critics of TRA champion racial "survival skills," cultural group preservation, and reciprocal obligations between black adults and individual black children based on racial community.

While I disagree with the policies advanced by the critics of TRA, their attention to race and racism underscores the practical need to address race as a factor in adoption. The likelihood that these race-conscious arguments will enhance racial justice in adoption is nonetheless attenuated by their inattention to individual agency in the process of racial self-identification. Individuals have a capacity and moral duty to actively respond to the racial categories they find themselves assigned to. We are social beings whose racial self-understandings affect social interaction. Passive absorption of racial classification promotes one-dimensional pictures of what it means to be white, black, Asian American, Latino/Latina, American Indian, and so on. Racial self-identification is better conceived as a never-ending process that varies from person to person and over a lifetime. Against this vision, the proponents of race-matching imagine a self not just affected by racial classification but overwhelmed by it.

Racial solidity—the idea that children should acquire a preset racial identity from parents who share their racial ascription—motivates much of the race-conscious opposition to TRA. Unlike racial solidarity, a strategic political alliance, racial solidity succumbs to a static notion of racial self-understanding. Advocates of racial solidity ground their opposition to TRA in three basic theoretical frames: cultural nationalism, multiculturalism, and communitarianism. What role does cultural nationalism play in the TRA debate? Can opposition to TRA be justified as a legitimate form of multiculturalism? Should public policy endorse same-race adoption as a form of cultural preservation? Does communitarianism support the assumption of an organic bond between black children and a black community? None of the scholars discussed in this chapter allies himself or herself with any one political theory. In this void, I have suggested three possible organizing frameworks. Together, these theories illuminate the primary concerns driving the vocal opposition to TRA, for each lens brings into focus a different aspect of racial imposition.

CULTURAL NATIONALISM

Cultural nationalism is one form of racial solidity found in scholarly criticisms of TRA. According to Michael Omi and Howard Winant, "In the nation-based paradigm, racial dynamics are understood as products of colonialism and, therefore, as outcomes of relationships which are global and epochal in character."[5] Black nationalism poses a counternarrative to colonial oppression in the form of national resistance. Black nationalists expand the idea of nation to encompass a diaspora held together by what Paul Gilroy calls "the Black Atlantic." National borders recognized by international law recede under the weight of a diffuse black or African nation that lacks physical borders. The Black Atlantic describes both the flow of people of African descent back and forth across the Atlantic Ocean (the Middle Passage, immigration, education, work, tourism) and the exchange of cultural artifacts and modes of life among black people living in various nation-states.[6]

Gilroy's metaphor of the Black Atlantic rejects the idea of culture as static possession. Rather, culture includes a wide range of practices and artifacts that change with time, location, and personal flare. Much of what is labeled "black culture" in the United States is more accurately described as the varied products of syncretism—the melding of disparate elements to create something new. Hip-hop, or example, is an ever-changing alchemy of disparate art forms plucked from syncopation, oral tradition, a simultaneous embracing and spoofing of crass U.S. commercialism, sampling from current and retro popular musical beats and lyrics, including rhythm and blues, funk, gospel, heavy metal, country music and more.[7] Though initially shaped by black and Latino/Latina youth living in the Bronx, hip-hop is not the exclusive province of those racial groups. Nobody owns it. Culture travels, and it changes according to where it's been and who picks it up. The cultural production of blacks living in Germany, Brazil, Nigeria, Canada, the United States, the United Kingdom, and in other dots in the Diaspora comprise a dynamic array of black international culture. This loosely tethered cultural backdrop creates a set of options; it does not predetermine the racial identification of any particular black person.

Cultural nationalism in the TRA debate defines black culture differently. Instead of seeing black culture as choice, advocates of racial solidity present black culture as fixed, "natural," and necessary for developing the right kind of racial self-understanding. This brand of cultural nationalism treats black children as passive receptacles of culture, cutting off the possibility that they could be active navigators of a wide assortment of cultural forms and styles of being that include but surpass the parameters of those practices that are culturally coded as "black." Critics of TRA tap a rich history of black nationalism in the

United States, dating back to the late eighteenth century.[8] Although present throughout U.S. history, black nationalism "tends to be most pronounced when the Negroes' status has declined, or when they have experienced intense disillusionment following a period of heightened but unfulfilled expectations."[9] Set in motion during the Revolutionary period, this cyclical trend began with elevated prospects for racial equality produced by the antislavery fervor that surrounded the American Revolution.[10] Such hopes evaporated with the framing of the first federal constitution in 1787, which explicitly recognized African slavery.[11] Then, in 1793, Congress passed the first fugitive slave law, issuing a mortal blow to any lingering hopes among blacks for equality with whites.[12] This trend would repeat itself cyclically, with black nationalist ideology resurfacing in the downturns.[13]

Scholarly objections to the placement of black children in white adoptive homes follow this historical trend. The initial response to increased numbers of TRA during the 1960s was linked to rhetorical appeals to racial separatism in the Black Power movement.[14] Many northern blacks were becoming frustrated with the civil rights movement's inability to ameliorate poverty and racist police brutality in northern cities such as Los Angeles, Detroit, Chicago, and Newark, where large numbers of African Americans had migrated. The Supreme Court, Congress, and three successive presidents worked to dismantle legal racism, eradicating all-white voting primaries in the South, knocking the legal teeth out of racially restrictive housing covenants, and removing official barriers that prevented black southerners from exercising their Fifteenth Amendment right to vote. More insidious forms of racism persisted, nevertheless, in the guise of racial profiling by police and store clerks and aversive racism in housing, education, and general social interaction.[15] Kwame Ture and Charles Hamilton use the term *institutional racism* to describe the tenacious forms of racism that have persisted long after the civil rights movement. Institutional racism refers to the anonymous ways in which social institutions perpetuate race-based inequalities in wealth, medical care, employment, and other key measures of life quality.[16] As many feminists remind us, institutional racism always operates in tandem with deep structures of sexism, as well as other modes of oppression and exclusion.[17]

Stereotypes that African Americans are less culturally evolved than whites further cloud the issue of racial inequality. Black cultural nationalism offers a counter to racially tinged culture of poverty political discourse. Culture refers to a pattern of human behavior, and the behavior of poor people has always attracted both the curiosity of the armchair anthropologist and the sincere interest of those who seek to alleviate poverty. Motivation matters but is frequently overshadowed by a mainstream cultural tendency to see the behavior of the black poor as pathological, as a product of race rather than as variegated responses to overarching social structure. Daniel Patrick Moynihan's 1965 U.S. Department of Labor study "The Negro Family: A Case for National Action" is a perfect example of good intentions gone awry. Moynihan reported that black female-headed families were a vestige of slavery and a key factor in high rates of unemployment for black men, as well as their disproportionately high rates of illegal drug use and school dropout rates. For Moynihan, this dire pattern signaled the need for more government intervention to repair historical damage dating back to slavery. But many seized on Moynihan's report for its caricature of black life that blamed black people for continuing to engage in socially "dysfunctional" behavior.[18] The worry is not without merit. Social conservatives have redirected Moynihan's unfortunate use of the phrase "tangle of pathology" (a term that Moynihan borrowed from the sociologist Kenneth Clark) to call for an end to the very kind of government social intervention that Moynihan recommended. Social and economic conservatives have argued that government welfare programs have spawned a culture of dependency that can only be corrected by eliminating such public policies. Some have described this as a form of "benign neglect," whereby the poor, who are disproportionately black and Latino/Latina, are left to change their "pathological behavior" on their own or with the aid of nongovernmental actors like churches.[19]

As with stereotypes generally, visions of welfare queens and dangerous young black males saturate all areas of U.S. life.[20] The real pathology is our collective inability to discuss government redress of racism without re-igniting malignant racial stereotypes in the process. One answer is to counter images of black cultural depravity with images of racial unity founded on positive cultural traditions. Cultural nationalists attempt precisely this when they construct counternarratives asserting that blacks are culturally equal, if not superior, to whites. Unlike revolutionary black nationalism that aims to overthrow existing political structure, "cultural nationalism has focused less on the political and economic elements of the nation-based approach than it has on *cultural* elements which give rise to collective identity, community, and a sense of 'people-hood.'"[21]

This strategy of cultural rehabilitation is nothing new. W. E. B. Du Bois's celebration of southern black folk culture in the aftermath of the Civil War can be read as a direct reply to Georg Friedrich Hegel's charge that Africa had no culture and thus "no historical part in the world."[22] Elaborating on Hegel's contention that the "spirit force" of nations moved history, Du Bois described the "spirit" of the Negro race as "the vastest and most ingenious invention for human progress." In "The Conservation of Races," Du Bois incorporates the Negro race into Hegel's theory of historical progress, where race defines "a vast family of human beings, generally of common blood and language, always of common history, traditions and impulses, who are both voluntarily and involuntarily striving together for the accomplishment of certain more or less vividly conceived ideals of life."[23]

Like all black cultural nationalists, Du Bois conflates culture, defined as a set of common traditions and impulses, with racial classification. And like many U.S. black cultural nationalists, Du Bois is often unclear about whether he is confining his discussion to blacks living in the United States or whether he is speaking of a geographically diverse racial diaspora. A person's racial classification and his cultural leanings may be related in practice, but the two ideas are conceptually distinct. Du Bois does say that the mutual pursuit of certain ideals is both a *voluntary* and involuntary enterprise. But this subtlety is shattered by the end result: He clearly believes that "race spirit" will lead each member of "the Negro race" to always reach for the same ideals, whether the individual is conscious of this organic racial impulse or not.

This false causal connection between race and culture supports many anti-TRA arguments. Ruth-Arlene Howe, for example, argues that black children belong in black adoptive homes because only black parents can give black children the right bundle of black "traditions and impulses." Howe formulates her black cultural nationalism in the following way: "What some scholars and policy makers seem to miss in their advocacy of TRA is that it is a form of 'cultural genocide.' Widespread, unregulated occurrences of private placements of infants of African American descent with non African American adoptive parents place these children at risk of alienation from their natural reference group. It poses a threat to the future vitality and unity of African Americans."[24] Buried in this harsh critique of TRA is a valid criticism of institutional racism in today's adoption system. Private, lawyer-mediated adoptions are increasingly popular and shield the racial preferences of prospective adopters from moral and legal scrutiny.

But Howe's critique of institutional racism is overshadowed by her description of black parents as a "natural reference group" for black children. The adjective *natural* connotes a presocial or prepolitical reality. More convincing is Charles Mills's argument that social contracts, both actual and imagined, invent racial categories as mechanisms of social and political exclusion.[25] We renew social contracts both explicitly and tacitly by our political decisions and our everyday social behavior. Racial navigation takes this political and social definition of race as a starting point for racial self-identification. Howe sees racial ascription as something far more intractable. Even if the language of nature is rhetorical, it still gives the misguided impression that racial categories predate civil society. Treating racial categories as natural makes it easier to draw a causal arrow between race and culture, and this in turn flattens the complexity of individuals. While racial categories give us existential starting blocks, each of us has his or her own course to run. If race is not synonymous with culture, then it follows that TRA cannot be a form of cultural genocide.

Even after deflating the hyperbolic language of cultural genocide, we still need to ask whether moderate race-matching can be justified on the grounds that racial navigation is more easily facilitated in an adoptive family where all family members share racial classification. James Bowen maintains that "a Black child's best interests entail being reared and socialized in the Black community." While Bowen concedes that TRA is preferable to institutional or foster care, he strongly supports race-matching, asserting that black adoptive parents are better equipped than white adoptive parents to teach black children how to "survive" the pressures of a racist society. Drawing a nexus between what he terms "Afro-American family values" and the best interests of black children *as a group*, Bowen insists that black survival skills can only be transmitted within a black family setting:

These survival devices include several learned abilities: to ignore (racial) insults; to decipher the appropriateness of fighting
back or submission; to emphasize Black strength, beauty and
worth as a countermeasure to the denigration of Blackness in
America; to rationalize Black shortcomings and failures as a
measure of discrimination and racism; to evaluate both objec-
tively and subjectively the level of nepotistic advantage or
same-group favoritism which precludes opportunities for advancement in education, employment or business.[26]

Survival, however, is not the major worry in adoption. The critical
question concerns the *quality* of life that a specific child is likely to experience with a specific parent or set of parents. Social workers should
place children in homes that are likely, in their professional estimation, to foster racial navigation. Racial navigation is a tool for coping
with racism that can be imparted by white adoptive parents as well as
by members of an extended family and the broader community. The
ability to be a creative problem-solver in a race-conscious society does
not depend on the racial composition of one's family. There is no one
prescription for a healthy racial self-concept. Assuming that black
children raised by white adoptive parents are necessarily deficient in
racial coping skills effectively pathologizes these individuals.[27] It pre-
judges them and their families as incompetent navigators of race.
    Still, if the protection of children from the harsh realities of racism
is a proper function of families, then maybe we should try harder to
place black children in black homes to ease their transition into social
life. This seems to be what Bowen is saying when he separates adoptive family life from "a social system where race is socially identified
and societally emphasized." Families, adoptive and original, are de-
picted as shelters under which black children will develop healthy
self-concepts that will in turn prepare them to handle racism in their
everyday social dealings. Longitudinal analyses such as the Rita
Simon–Howard Altstein twenty-year study of transracially adoptive
families assuage this worry, concluding that black adoptees raised in
white homes are "aware of and comfortable with their racial identity."[28] Yet, DeBerry, Scarr, and Weinberg find that black children who
are raised in white adoptive families encounter unique stressors that
make it difficult for them to adjust to certain situations that require a
black or what they term "Africentric" ecological competence.[29] In ad-

dition to the mixed outcomes of child developmental studies of TRA, many of the studies suffer from research design flaws that further cloud their results. It is difficult, perhaps impossible, to measure whether TRA is "good" or "bad" for black children.

A more powerful response to Bowen's concern may be to point out that families cannot completely shield children from social forces. In Arlene Skolnick's words: "The family is a place of enduring bonds and fragile relationships, of the deepest love and the most intractable conflicts, of the most intense passions and the routine tedium of everyday life. It is a shelter from the workings of a harsh economy, and it is battered beyond its control."[30] Families are rightly conceived as shelters, but there is no evidence that a same-race family will do a better job of fending off the forces of racism than will an interracial family. A more pragmatic approach would be to envision families as social institutions where race and racism can be discussed in a safe and caring manner.

This vision of family life supports the idea that racial navigation is to begin in one's childhood. Children are immature persons dependent on adults for their care needs and political representation. As Martha Minow comments, "Deferring to parents, rather than to individual children, does stand as the one nearly universal exception from the Constitution's commitment to individual self-determination."[31] Even if children are not capable of self-determination in the fullest sense, they are nonetheless on the road to and thus in the process of fashioning their self-concepts. This seemingly obvious point—that children are potential adults—is routinely overlooked in the TRA debate, as both sides focus on initial placement decisions. Adoption policy should reflect both the specific care needs of individual children and consider them as future adults. Families can and should protect children from many of life's blows, but families should not try to inoculate children from the social significance of race. Instead, parents should teach their children to distinguish between third-person racial ascription and first-person racial self-identification as a way to ward off the pressure of racial stereotypes of themselves and others.

Inattention to individual agency in the arguments against TRA is symptomatic of the polemical structure of black nationalism generally. The idea of reproduction figures prominently in these counternarratives. Cultural nationalists stress the importance of ensuring the future vitality of a metaphysical nation through figurative and literal reproduction. This is not to deny the existence of various black geographical communities or a national sense of race-based solidarity within the United States. The problem is that cultural nationalists insist on a set of cultural prerequisites for admission to a narrowly conceived "national" community, rather than allowing for a culturally diverse community of persons to form on the basis of common racial ascription. Human reproduction symbolizes both metaphysical nation-building and the perpetuation of cultural practice. Hence, culture becomes the raw material for "nation-building," and the racially solid "nation" then becomes a shield against perceived threats to the survival of "the black community." The threat to the black community cannot refer to the physical existence of blacks as a minority group within the United States because the number of black children adopted by whites is relatively tiny: "The black community within this nation is not threatened with extinction. The number of black children available for adoption is very small compared to the size of the black community; placing more of those available for adoption transracially poses no realistic threat to the existence of that community or the preservation of its culture."[32]

It is easy to see how same-race adoption fits into this story. Dorothy Roberts writes, "Black parents transmit to their children their own cultural identity and teach them to defy racist stereotypes and practices, training them to live in two cultures, both Black and white."[33] Parents teach their children their values and cultural practices. Indeed, a virtue of family life in the United States is being exposed to a subset of the tremendous variety of cultural practices that constitute a broader U.S. culture. Martha Minow argues that "parents' opportunity for self-definition should include control over their children's identities, but public power should be deployed to open children's chances to invent themselves, and to overcome the segregation effect of past generations' choices."[34] Minow's attempt to strike a balance between self-invention and providing legal remedies for group-based injustices is salutary, but parental control over children's racial identities is misapplied in the case of TRA. It might make sense to speak of children as extensions of their parents' self-definition in the area of religious affiliation, where there is an option to abandon such practices on reaching adulthood. But race has a different kind of social salience. Race has a visual dimension that few can elude. Rather than predetermining a child's racial self-concept, parents should encourage children to develop their own racial self-understanding. At the same time, parents ought to practice what they preach and critically reflect on their own racial self-identifications. As part of racial navigation, adopted children should be given the opportunity to "consult" their original and adoptive families in a lifelong process of revising their self-understanding. This consultation need not refer to a physical meeting or actual contact. Consultation can refer simply to an adopted person's access to nonidentifying information about his or her original family including their racial classification. Searching for original family members can also fit into this broad notion of consultation. Regardless of whether original family members are found, and how those reunions turn out, the looking alone is instrumental in piecing together one's story.

Anti-TRA arguments that portray black adults as proprietors of black culture vis-à-vis parental control over black children crush the autonomy of adoptees. Rather than expressing genuine concern for the best interests of individual black children, as legally mandated,[35] advocates of racial solidity insist that the placement of black children in black adoptive homes is necessary for the proper transmission of black culture and a solid racial identity: "Since Blacks as a group are embattled," the argument goes, "the loss of [their] children threatens the entire group, not just the individuals."[36] Twila Perry worries that "black children raised by white parents may fail to identify with the Black Community and will, accordingly, be lost as a resource to that community."[37] This statement betrays a major problem with applying cultural nationalism to adoption policy: the use of black children to further adult conceptions of racial community or "nation."

As noted earlier, black cultural nationalism tries to counteract the stereotype that blacks lack cultural sophistication and thus cannot measure up to whites. In this vein, Harold Cruse sees black cultural nationalism as "nothing more than a strategic retreat for a purpose. It proposes to change, not the white world outside, but the black world inside."[38] Internal address is a prominent feature of many black nationalist statements, and Cruse is right to flag this rhetorical posture. While whites are never the primary audience for black nationalism, they are almost always meant to *overhear* these "manifestoes of identity."[39]

It is one thing to use racial retreat as rhetorical strategy and quite another to transport cultural nationalism into a tense and highly symbolic public policy debate like TRA. Successful political arguments couched in black cultural nationalism are especially pernicious because they stamp race essentialism with a legal seal of approval.

MULTICULTURALISM

An alternative interpretation of the theoretical arguments against TRA is one based in multiculturalism. Like cultural nationalism, multicultural arguments treat culture as a group possession worth preserving. But unlike the internal address of cultural nationalism, multicultural advocates typically promote the idea of cultural exchange between and among different groups as a social good. Applying a multicultural framework to the TRA debate prompts the question, "Are black adults morally justified in opposing the placement of black children in white homes based on the preservation of a black cultural group for the purpose of multicultural exchange?" Before answering this question we will need to be certain that we are not confusing multiculturalism with political theories of cultural pluralism that fail to tackle the issue of cultural interplay. For instance, while both Michael Walzer's "politics of difference" and Charles Taylor's "politics of recognition" have been discussed as multicultural arguments, neither offers a theory of *how* group interaction is to occur after cultural pluralism has been established. Lawrence Blum's argument for anti-racist multicultural education addresses the inter-cultural aspect that is assumed but rarely addressed in political theory. Because the difference between cultural pluralism and multiculturalism is so often overlooked, and so important for racial justice in adoption, I shall take a closer look at the work of Walzer, Taylor, and Blum.

The "Politics of Difference"
In the essay collection *What It Means to Be an American*, Michael Walzer sets out to give "a comparative and theoretical account of the politics of difference and suggest how it might work in social settings where immigration and cultural pluralism are already and where they aren't yet of major importance."[40] In the case of the United States, Walzer's "politics of difference" is to describe how "cultural diversity" has come about. With no explicit discussion of intercultural exchange, Walzer's "politics of difference" is more a theory of cultural

pluralism than a model of multiculturalism. He avoids the issue of U.S. racism, thus leaving unanswered the "harder question" of how blacks and "black culture" may or may not fit into the "politics of difference" model.[41] No serious analysis of U.S. multiculturalism can sidestep the issue of racism and racial difference because the idea of race is so central to what it means to be an American. Does racial difference constitute just another "difference" in a theory of cultural pluralism such as Walzer's? And can such a theory of cultural pluralism be transformed into a morally just basis for race-matching adoption policy?

Walzer's politics of difference is modeled after "American success stories" of ethnic pluralism and religious toleration. American cultural diversity is celebrated without explaining cultural pluralism's failure to incorporate black Americans in the same manner as ethnic and religious groups. Three pivotal moments mark a "politics of difference" road to political incorporation. First, a group that has been repressed, fearful, and invisible articulates its existence as a distinct entity and demands public recognition of both its members' solidarity and the group's value within the society. At this point of articulation, the group "can no longer be denied, abolished, assimilated, or transcended. It is simply *there*, a feature of the social world, and from now on any refusal to recognize it will itself be recognized as an act of oppression."[42]

This stage is "cacophonous" and will need to be negotiated.[43] In the negotiation phase, the limits of one group's legitimate claims are set by the legitimate claims of other groups. Domestically, such negotiation may take the form of limited access to public funds based on, for example, the constitutional "wall" separating religious beliefs from state support.[44] And from this point, groups work toward the final moment of incorporation, which is difficult to carry out in practice as the First Amendment example suggests. Fragments resulting from the articulation and negotiation stages are brought together in the ideal of a nonrepressive "universe of difference"—a process that must entail economic assistance and political cooperation.

Racism stalls African American group claims at the first stage of Walzer's trajectory: articulation of the group's distinctness, its solidarity, and above all its value in a world of other group claims. Would race-matching adoption policies help blacks get over this hurdle?

Maybe. But publicly valued racial solidarity can be accomplished in more just and effective ways than race-matching adoption policies. A better strategy for asserting the social value of blackness would stress the need for a moral principle of nondiscrimination in the crafting of adoption policy, as discussed in Chapter 2. Even if cultural pluralism could justify arguments against TRA, there remains the question of whether the particular experiences of African Americans can be accommodated by cultural pluralism at all. Although he doesn't discuss racism in any detail, Walzer does say that African American group claims have sometimes moved beyond the first stage of pluralist incorporation. He points to race-based affirmative action programs as evidence that racism is not an insurmountable obstacle on the road to pluralist success.[45] Recent judicial rollbacks of affirmative action programs nonetheless demonstrate the precarious state of this path to African American incorporation.[46]

Contrary to the insistence of neoconservative intellectuals like Thomas Sowell and Nathan Glazer, race does not equal ethnicity in America.[47] African Americans are not just another ethnic group in a sea of ethnic pluralism. It is even doubtful that the popularization of the term *African American* by many blacks during the 1980s signaled any sincere ethnic ambitions, as Walzer suggests it might have.[48] Toni Morrison argues that blackness or, more pointedly, "Africanism" marks the edges of the dominant white American community: "Africanism is the vehicle by which the American self knows itself as not enslaved, but free; not repulsive, but desirable; not helpless, but licensed and powerful; not history-less, but historical; not damned, but innocent; not a blind accident of evolution, but the progressive fulfillment of destiny."[49] Morrison's point is not to deny the existence of racial diversity beyond the black–white divide. Instead, she uses the novels of Willa Cather, James Joyce, Gertrude Stein and others to show how the whiteness or racelessness of the protagonist is often formed by the presence of marginal black characters. Morrison's literary insight captures the fictionality of race in the United States. Still, one must acknowledge the power of this fiction, for it produces profound experiential consequences, both materially and psychologically.[50]

Contemporary U.S. society is more complicated than the duality of whiteness and blackness suggests. As historian Ronald Takaki comments, "One of the lessons of the Los Angeles explosion is the recognition of the fact that we are a multiracial society and that race can no longer be defined in the binary terms of black and white."[51] Yet equally true is the reality that in our multiethnic society, nonwhite ethnic minorities' chances of political incorporation are affected by the persistent racial exclusion of blacks. Takaki acknowledges, for example, that the Asian American Janus-faced stereotype of "model minority" and overly studious "nerd" is both used to discipline blacks (chastising them for their "laziness") and justify admissions quotas for Asian Americans seeking higher education.[52] Nonwhite ethnic minorities are caught in this web of racial exclusion. Their prospects for successfully negotiating the "politics of difference" are alternately dimmed and lit by the racial exclusion of blacks.

The "Politics of Recognition"

This web of racial exclusion prevents nonwhites from being perceived as fully American, thus denying these individuals proper recognition. Charles Taylor diagnoses this failure to properly recognize someone as one of our modern ailments. In premodern times, when honor was based on one's station in a social hierarchy, questions of recognition never arose. One was born a prince or a pauper, and social mobility was not expected. The "politics of recognition" became a central pinning of our personal and public identity understandings when the egalitarian concept of dignity replaced that of honor at the end of the eighteenth century.[53] Moreover, "what has come about with the modern age is not the need for recognition but the conditions in which the attempt to be recognized can fail."[54] The promise of due or proper recognition by others propels models of cultural pluralism and multiculturalism. It is not enough that a group be recognized in a nonrepressive politics of difference. The group must be *properly* recognized. It must be valued in the right way. Misrecognition, as in the case of negative racial and gender stereotyping, "can inflict harm, can be a form of oppression, imprisoning someone in a false, distorted, and reduced mode of being."[55]

On this point, Taylor takes his cues from the Martinique-born psychiatrist Frantz Fanon, whose theoretical accounts of African liberation from colonial rule continue to illuminate our understanding of racial subordination.[56] Fanon defined racial subjugation as the imposition of inferior self-images on colonized blacks. Borrowing the idea of overdetermination from Jean-Paul Sartre, Fanon writes,

> I am overdetermined from without. I am the slave not of the "idea" that others have of me but of my own appearance. . . . I am being dissected under white eyes, the only real eyes. I am *fixed*. Having adjusted their microtomes, they objectively cut away slices of my reality. I am laid bare. I feel, I see in those white faces that it is not a new man who has come in, but a new kind of man, a new genus. Why, it's a Negro![57]

In this famous passage, Fanon's phenotype, his appearance under white eyes, is like a jail sentence. The colonial relationship between oppressor and oppressed—a relationship visibly marked by skin color—sets the stage for identity struggle. Fanon was convinced that violent revolt against one's colonizers was necessary to strip away the imprint of a degrading self-image: "To shoot down a European is to kill two birds with one stone, to destroy an oppressor and the man he oppresses, at the same time: there remain a dead man, and a free man."[58] Fanon's liberation framework, read metaphorically, can help to explain various efforts by African Americans to rework the negative life scripts given to them by the white majority.[59] If overdetermination inflicts metaphysical wounds, "one form of healing the self that those who have these identities participate in is learning to see these collective identities not as sources of limitation and insult but as a valuable part of what they centrally are."[60]

Taylor discusses the issue of political recognition in the context of whether the Canadian government should recognize Quebec as a "distinct society" under cultural siege from a cultural (linguistic) majority: "Policies aimed at survival actively seek to create members of the community, for instance, in their assuring that future generations continue to identify as French-speakers."[61] The goal of cultural continuation may be reasonable; however, one can value cultural differences and simultaneously set limits on the means used to facilitate the perpetuation of particular cultural practices. Adult members of groups may encourage children to identify with the group and carry on its cultural practices, but adults are not morally justified in dictating the racial self-identification of children.

Will Kymlicka offers a more flexible theory of the nexus between community and cultural practice by presenting culture as an array of options made available to individuals in the hope that they might achieve a deeper self-understanding: "This understanding of cultural membership doesn't involve any necessary connection with the shared ends which characterize the culture at any given moment. The primary good being recognized is the cultural community as a context of choice, not the character of the community or its traditional ways of life, which people are free to endorse or reject."[62] This dialogical identity construction, endorsed by both Taylor and Kymlicka, respects the individual agency of black individuals in selecting their cultural endeavors. In Taylor's words, "We define our identity always in dialogue with, sometimes in struggle against, the things our significant others want to see in us."[63] I prefer to use the adjective *dialogical* to describe our relationships with nonintimate others, saving *conversational* to portray the intimate relationships of family life.

Kymlicka's idea of contexts of choice comes closer than Walzer and Taylor in promoting intercultural exchange because it invites people to pick cultural artifacts and practices from a broad array of options. But even Kymlicka's context of choice reads more like a recipe for cultural pluralism than a sincere push for cultural interaction and exchange among subnational groups. Multiculturalism requires that people share cultural practices with one another in a way that challenges racism, ethnocentrism, sexism, homophobia, and religious intolerance. Real multiculturalism makes us confront our own prejudices and anxieties about otherness. Walzer, Taylor, and Kymlicka do not confront the exclusion of African Americans from the ethnic and religious models of political incorporation.

Lawrence Blum builds his theory of multiculturalism around the need for an explicit anti-racist moral imperative, thereby reviving the implicit promise of multiculturalism—positive inter-group contact that aims to combat negative stereotyping. Blums writes: "Especially in the United States, notions of cultural respect and pluralism are much more widely known and accepted than 'antiracism'; indeed the latter notion carries an unfamiliar or somewhat threatening, confrontative, and 'radical' connotation that 'respect for different cultures' does not."[64] Although tolerance is better than intolerance, antiracism contributes much more to the social good. Antiracist multiculturalism promotes personal introspection through critical dialogue with others. It also differentiates between race and culture, reminding us that racial categories do not determine a person's cultural attachments and practices. Although Blum's anti-racist theory of multiculturalism values African American group-based identity, he does not perceive this distinctiveness as a barrier in family life or social life. On the contrary, his argument encourages TRA. But we need to be careful here. Just as multiculturalism does not substantiate objections to TRA, neither should multiculturalism be advanced on its own as a suitable justification of TRA. Black children awaiting adoption should not be viewed as representatives of "black culture" saddled with the burden of teaching their adoptive parents about African American group identity. An immense power imbalance exists between children and adults in families based on age and care needs. White adoptive parents of black children should be encouraged to seek multicultural exchange with black *adults* based on *mutual* sharing and discomfort that works to avoid superficiality.

A Communitarian Defense of TRA?
While most communitarian political theories do not explicitly challenge racism, the communitarian effort to reconcile "individual rights and community needs" may be a more hospitable ground for racial navigation than either cultural nationalism, cultural pluralism, or multiculturalism. Indeed, communitarianism can be stretched to accommodate racial navigation even though race is conspicuously absent from most communitarian arguments. But this flexibility also indicates that communitarianism may not be very different from the liberal arguments its proponents have so intently criticized. The definition of community at the heart of communitarian political theory is elastic. Amitai Etzioni says that communities are "webs of social relations that encompass shared meaning and above all shared values," adding that "families may qualify as mini-communities."[65]

Adoption involves two layers of family association—original and adoptive which may or may not be racially or otherwise similar. How, if at all, should a child's original family and original community attachments affect adoption policy and practice? The communitarian critique of liberalism objects to hyperindividualistic rights talk that imagines a self apart from community-based connection. Michael Sandel, Mary Ann Glendon, Jean Bethke Elshtain, and others argue that liberalism exaggerates individual autonomy, thus minimizing the descriptive weight of community-based identity and obligation. If the descriptive theory is wrong, then the prescriptive theory is likely to be wrong, too, because it will not resonate with most people's self-understanding.[66] Yet these self-described critics of liberalism do not provide "a settled sense about the *scope* and *scale* of the social entity that they have in mind."[67] Does racial community shape us in the same way as religious, ethnic, or geographical community? The kind of community makes a moral difference. Being a Catholic is different from being a South-Asian American because the latter involves immutable physical features that carry a social meaning that cannot be abandoned at will. Contemporary Catholicism in the United States is not a proxy for race, and people are free to leave the Catholic Church and join other religious denominations and faiths, or they can reject organized religion altogether. Likewise, Americans are free to convert to Catholicism by undergoing a strict process of education and initiation. As Mary Lyndon Shanley rightly concludes, communitarians misunderstand "the liberal commitment, which is not to self prior to any ends whatsoever but to a self whose ends are neither imposed from without nor exempt from reexamination."[68]

Shanley argues that the 1978 Indian Child Welfare Act (ICWA) exemplifies this liberal commitment by taking a child's racial community attachments into account without locking that child into a fixed racial category. There are two major parts of the ICWA: First, tribes maintain jurisdiction over adoption and foster care proceedings involving child members of the tribe who have been domiciled on the reservation. And tribes have the right to be notified of adoption and foster care cases involving nondomiciled child members of the tribe. Second, in state adoption and foster care proceedings, "a preference shall be given, in the absence of good cause to the contrary, to the placement with (1) a member of the child's extended family; (2) other members of the Indian child's tribe; or (3) other Indian families." Finally, the ICWA allows for the original parents' preferences to be "considered" in placement decisions when "appropriate."[69]

The Multiethnic Placement Act, as amended in 1996 (MEPA II), exempts "Indian" as the only racial/ethnic category that may be explicitly and routinely considered by federally funded adoption agencies. Why sanction race-matching in the case of Indians and not blacks? There are key differences between the political and legal status of Indians and that of black Americans based on different historical experiences of racism. While both racial groups have historically suffered de jure racial discrimination and continue to encounter institutional racism, only American Indian children were systematically removed from their homes in large numbers and placed in white foster and adoptive homes.[70] Hence the ICWA is a remedial measure designed to rectify a specific and recent historical wrong. The historical injury suffered by blacks in adoption has been in the form of legal and extralegal exclusion from adoption and foster care services. With MEPA II, the government aims to rectify this particular injustice by abolishing policies that mandate racial segregation in adoptive placement.

Shanley disarms the communitarian critique of liberalism by showing that the ICWA is consistent with a more contextual or community-sensitive liberalism that views individuals as being influenced by various communities but not wholly or fundamentally defined by their community affiliations. Individual civil rights are crucial, both symbolically and strategically, but people are more than just rights-holders; they are members of multiple and sometimes overlapping communities and social contexts. Shanley's liberalism recognizes that children awaiting adoption are not blank slates, no matter how young they are. Original parents and their racial identifications affect the lives of adopted individuals even in the absence of personal information and physical contact. The difficult question is, "How do we make these contextual factors legally and practically relevant in specific cases of adoption?"

Explicit racial preferences should not be a matter of routine agency policy. But, as I argued in Chapter 2, social workers should be permitted to evaluate how the broader context of a race-conscious social structure might affect *individual* children in their particular circumstances, including their racial ascription and the racial ascription of their potential adoptive parents. This is a necessary step in contemplating the best interests of individual children, and such extralegal racial consideration is consistent with both the letter and spirit of MEPA II. For American Indian children in need of adoption, the jurisdictional component of the ICWA is morally just because Indians have a unique legal relationship to federal and state law, and because ceding jurisdictional authority in adoption and foster care aims to rectify a discrete historical denial of this authority. I disagree, however, with the racial preference component of the ICWA, especially the proviso that original parents may "when appropriate" express a placement preference that may be race-based.

The ICWA does not say when such consideration is "appropriate" or how such parental preferences would affect actual placement decisions. Though Shanley does not say that original parents (mostly mothers) should be allowed to determine or even seriously influence placement decisions concerning their children, she does say "it might make sense for the parent *to be heard* with respect to placement." Shanley wants to give original parents a voice in adoption as a way of countering both the historical secrecy that has defined so much U.S. adoption policy and practice and the subtext that all women who relinquish their children for adoption are bad mothers. Instead of stereotyping original mothers as social deviants, Shanley asks us to rethink the act of giving up a child for adoption "as part of an effort to provide care for one's offspring."[71]

Original mothers are often excluded from discussion about adoption policy and practice. Women surrender their children for a variety of reasons, many of which can be traced to sincere care. But I am wary of according original parents formal influence over placement decisions even in the case of American Indians. Granting original parents formal power over placement decisions opens the door for them to discriminate against prospective adopters on the basis of race, religion, geographical location, socioeconomic status, and so on.[72] Social workers may take the wishes of original parents into consideration informally as part of a larger assessment of a child's best interests. Indeed, many social workers do allow original parents "to be heard" and have been doing so for a long time. Giving original parents a formal say in adoption is not necessary for promoting racial navigation in adoptive families. If racial navigation is to be facilitated, a child needs to have access to some information about his original family and original communities. This information adds choices to an adopted child's context of choice, which is also shaped by her adoptive family's racial composition and cultural practices. In this way, original parents can and should have an indirect, rather than direct, effect on the lives of the children they make available for adoption.

Racial classifications impose constraints on all individuals living in a race-conscious society. But all racial designations are not created equal. Economic inequality, social capital fueling old-boy and now old-girl networks, and the psychological blinders that make some people appear less human than others create and sustain a profoundly unequal social landscape. Talking about racism is frustrating because discourse about race tends to oscillate between the two poles of colorblindness and permanent racial retreat, both of which shut down conversation and dialogue. Advocates of colorblindness attempt to linguistically level the playing field. In doing so, they deprive the victims of racism of a language to articulate their injury. Mere mention of race-consciousness spawns cries of "reverse racism," as whites hunker down for the expected onslaught of black militancy.

Everyone must navigate racial categories because these categories go to the heart of what it means to be an American. Transracial adoption throws our optimism about race relations into the face of hard realities that test the mettle of individual families. Navigating racial categories and the communities they produce is practically necessary. The anti-TRA arguments explored in this chapter endorse a theory of racial solidity—the simplistic premise that race is a bundle of cultural practices to be handed down from black parents to black children. My objection is not that these scholars take a race-conscious approach to adoption. It is, rather, their definition of racial identity and community that troubles me. While critics of TRA do not insist that black children should be relegated to foster care if the only option for placement is with white adoptive parents, they all assert that a "moderated" policy of race-matching is in the best interests of all black children awaiting adoption. By "moderated" they mean policies that give preference to same-race placement over interracial placement. We need the broad-based principles of antidiscrimination and racial navigation to produce racially just outcomes in adoption. Neither side in the TRA debate has built a comprehensive notion of racial justice in adoption because both sides lack a conception of adopted individuals as active navigators of racial meanings. This book is an effort to resuscitate this racial agency. In the next chapter, I present a thought experiment that uses these theoretical tools to imagine a comprehensive picture of a racially just system of adoption.

CHAPTER 4
Racial Randomization

In the novel *Edgar Allen*, a white middle-class American family adopts a black boy and then returns him to the adoption agency, unable to cope with the racist pressures of their community. As Edgar Allen's white adoptive brother observes, "The funny things were nothing you could get upset about, really. But every once in a while a crazy kind of look from people in a passing car, or a little extra room around our blankets at the beach. That sort of thing. I guess people were just startled by seeing the five of us playing with the one of E. A. [Edgar Allen], and behaving as though we all belonged together."[1] Race-based assumptions about which persons belong together in families run deep in our social ontology. Transracial adoption has the potential to challenge both the normative weight of same-race family structure and the flawed assumption that strong and meaningful family bonds require a genetic tie.

Supporters of TRA argue that race-matching policies violate the Fourteenth Amendment rights of prospective adopters not to be subject to state-sponsored racial discrimination. Those opposed to TRA maintain that race-matching is a constitutionally permissible form of group preservation. With the exception of legal scholar Richard Banks, neither side of the debate has defended the Fourteenth Amendment rights of prospective adoptive children to be chosen without state-sponsored racial bias.[2] Moral inquiry into adoption policy should be expanded to address the full range of invidious racial discrimination in adoption.

A comprehensive application of equal-protection law in adoption would prevent prospective adopters from selecting children based on racial classification. While Banks recommends implementation of such a policy, I present "racial randomization" as a thought experiment designed to tweak our moral intuitions about nondiscrimination. These moral intuitions are crucial because they guide social workers and prospective adopters in their interpretation of adoption policies. The 1994 Multiethnic Placement Act (MEPA), amended in 1996, prohibits federally funded adoption agencies from using the race of prospective adopters or children to delay or deny a placement decision. MEPA aims to guard against state-sponsored invidious racial discrimination, but social workers and prospective parents should be cognizant that a child's racial ascription will affect how others treat her and thus how she views herself. As I argued in Chapter 2, race-sensitivity is both permissible under MEPA and salutary for it bridges the gap between public and private realms of racial meaning. A fine line often exists between racial awareness and racial discrimination, a division that categorical legal language on its own cannot maintain. We need an additional set of moral arguments that prompt us to reflect on the personal dimensions of racial meaning that all of us bring to the public event of adoption. The thought experiment of racial randomization is designed to accomplish this goal by supplementing the legal principle of nondiscrimination with a broad-based moral principle of nondiscrimination that challenges the widespread assumption that we are morally justified in configuring our families based on racial choice. The resistance that racial randomization is likely to provoke, even as hypothical, exposes the tenacity of de facto racial segregation in the American family.

Despite increased numbers of interracial marriage and partnerships, most American families continue to be racially homogeneous. Biologism, the idea that adoptive families should resemble biologically based families, transfers this presumption of racially exclusive family structure to the adoption world and is evidenced by the extremely low numbers of TRAs. Rita Simon and Rhonda Roorda estimate that the number of adoptions that involved white parents and black children in 1999 may be as low as 1.2 percent.[3] Race-based aversion is widespread in today's adoption system. In 1994, black children comprised an estimated 52.3 percent of all U.S. children awaiting adoption, up from 50.3 percent in 1993. White children comprised about 42.6 percent of all children awaiting adoption in 1994, down from 47.6 percent in 1993.[4] Most adopters are white (about 67 percent).[5] Blacks adopt at higher rates than their white counterparts, controlling for socioeconomic class, and also adopt informally at much higher rates than whites.[6] But even so, there are not enough black adopters to adopt all the black children in need of adoption. White adopters generally request healthy domestic white infants (or DWIs, or HWIs as they are sometimes referred to in adoption world vernacular), and many are willing to spend large amounts of money and personal energy to achieve that goal.[7]

The scant attention given to the race-based decisions of prospective adopters is connected to strong cultural attachments to the idea of privacy—attachments that are grounded in judicial constructions of the U.S. Constitution. This cultural attachment does not mean, however, that familial privacy has been consistently applied in practice. Antimiscegenation laws were constitutional until 1967.[8] And even today, antisodomy laws that are selectively used to prosecute gays and lesbians for sexual conduct that may take place in the context of a committed relationship remain constitutional. Moreover, the legal institution of marriage continues to be closed to any relationship other than one man and one woman. Adoption is a legal and social practice that involves both state-sponsored public decision-making and the privacy of familial association. As a matter of family law, adoption falls within the police powers of individual states. In order to formalize or legalize an adoption, a court must transfer parental rights from the original parents to the adopters, administer changes to the adopted child's birth certificate, and legalize any name changes. This state involvement is limited to the placement process, during which the state is entrusted to promote the best interests of individual children in need of permanent homes.

But adoption is more than just the moment of legal placement. Placement decisions initiate a long-term and intimate association of family life—an association we typically regard as private. The necessary involvement of the state in the construction of adoptive families attenuates, but does not destroy, the constitutionally sanctioned privacy we expect in the formation of families. None of this is to say that adoptive families are not "real families" or that once placement has occurred these families do not deserve the same privacy rights accorded to other families. Rather, the case study of TRA shows that private race-based preferences and race-based social aversion are interlocked.

RACIAL RANDOMIZATION

Adoption is a unique social institution. Unlike traditional biological reproduction, adoption requires that government coordinate the interests of three parties: the original parent(s), the child, and the adopters. Hence the catch-phrase "adoption triangle" or "adoption triad." This state involvement is a form of state action and is therefore arguably subject to the Fourteenth Amendment's ban on state-sponsored racial discrimination. Richard Banks calls the racial classification of children by adoption agencies "facilitative accommodation":

> When engaged in by public agencies, facilitative accommodation, like race matching is an instance of race-based state action. In both cases, adoption agencies racially classify children. Through race matching, the state mandates the placement of children with parents on the basis of race. Through facilitative accommodation, the state's racial classification promotes the race-based decision-making of prospective adoptive parents by framing the choice of a child in terms of race, encouraging parents to consider children based on the ascribed characteristic of race rather than individually. In both cases, a court, in finalizing the adoption, validates the actions of the adoption agency.[9]

The invidious consequence of facilitative accommodation is that "most black children in need of adoption are categorically denied, on the basis of their race, the opportunity to be considered individually for adoption by the majority of prospective adoptive parents."[10] In Banks's view, public adoption agencies should stop classifying children based on race to safeguard the equal-protection rights of children in need of adoption. He calls this policy proposal "strict nonaccommodation."

Although our arguments share a constitutional basis, Banks and I differ quite dramatically in the scope of our application. Strict nonaccommodation is an actual policy proposal, whereas racial randomization is a thought experiment designed to motivate adoption practitioners and prospective adopters to question their own racial biases and expectations, and how such prejudice may conflict with the moral rights of children awaiting adoption not to be discriminated against on the basis of their racial ascription. The goal is to bring the legal principle of nondiscrimination into alignment with a moral principle of nondiscrimination applied to behavior we think of as private. Banks wants to implement strict nonaccommodation within the current adoption system, whereas racial randomization imagines a new adoption system. Banks would exempt black prospective adopters from strict nonaccommodation. In contrast, the hypothetical of racial randomization applies to all would-be adopters.

Imagine an adoption system consisting solely of centralized public adoption agencies within individual states. This system is the only option available to those who wish to become adoptive parents. In this adoption system, applicants must undergo a screening process during which each is informed of the agency's policy of discounting race as a permissible preference in being matched with a child who needs a home. If an applicant agrees to this policy, he or she continues the screening process for a minimum level of parental fitness. If all goes well, then he or she is approved to become an adoptive parent. In the randomization process, some white applicants will be matched with black children, and some black applicants will be matched with white children, while some from both groups will end up adopting children of the same racial classification as their own. Whites are statistically likely to be matched with a black child through a system of racial randomization. And it is probable that a small number of white children will be placed with black parents.

The adoption of white children by black parents would be a beneficial consequence of racial randomization because it would highlight the unilateral racial aspect of TRA. It would call into question the racist presumption that interracial care is unidirectional in family life, that whites adopt black children but black adults can only care for white children as domestic workers.[11] Kim McLarin, a writer and the black mother of a light-skinned biracial daughter, recounts the refusal of whites to see her as the biological mother of a "white"–looking child. Remembering a visit to a white pediatrician, McLarin writes,

> The doctor took one look at Samantha and exclaimed: "Wow! She's so light!" I explained that my husband is white, but it didn't seem to help. The doctor commented on Sam's skin color so often that I finally asked what was on her mind. "I'm thinking albino," she said. The doctor, who is white, claimed that she had seen the offspring of many interracial couples, but never a child this fair. "They're usually darker, coffee-with-cream color. Some of them are this light at birth, but by 72 hours you can tell they have a black parent." To prove her point, she held her arm next to Samantha's stomach. "I mean, this could be my child!"[12]

The pediatrician did not challenge Ms. McLarin's parenting ability in any direct way. Yet what are we to make of her disbelief that contrasting skin tones could represent a mother and daughter? The pediatrician's lapse in professional decorum is linked to deep-seated stereotypes of black neediness and white superiority. The possibility that racial randomization would match some black parents with white children forces us to confront some of the race-based expectations we collectively hold about which people belong together in a family.

STRICT NONACCOMMODATION: "WHITES ONLY"

Banks's policy of strict nonaccommodation would in principle exempt black prospective adopters, who would be free to exercise race-based preferences in the selection of adoptive children.[13] Banks brackets the racial attitudes of black adopters for two reasons. First, the same-race adoptive preferences of blacks have a negligible effect on our social terrain, while those of whites will exacerbate existing racial inequalities; second, the adoption of black children by blacks advances the social good of cultural pluralism, while the adoption of white children by whites does not.

Banks is right to be particularly concerned about revising the racial attitudes of whites in the adoption system. Whites constitute the majority of adopters, and their same-race adoptive choices are routinely overlooked, as public attention turns to highly publicized cases of "reverse discrimination" in which whites' efforts to adopt black children are thwarted.[14] But one can be concerned with revising the racial attitudes of white adopters and still find reasons to include black adopters in hypothetical racial randomization. As discussed above, one reason to include blacks in racial randomization is the social utility gained by the otherwise unlikely outcome of some blacks adopting white children. If blacks typically choose black children when they adopt, then TRAs involving black parents and white or other nonblack children are likely to only occur under randomization. Such adoptions challenge racist stereotypes about the direction of interracial care.

Banks defends his exemption of blacks from strict nonaccommodation on the grounds of cultural pluralism. He believes that "our society has an important interest in maintaining cultural diversity." To further this social goal, blacks and other racial minorities are justified in using racial preferences in adoption to promote their cultural presence in the society.[15] He tries to avoid collapsing the idea of race into culture, but ultimately cannot divorce his cultural defense of same-race black preferences from cultural nationalist arguments in favor of race-matching, that were examined in Chapter 3. A cultural defense of same-race adoption for blacks fastens the link between racial ascription and cultural practice too tightly. While race and culture may be related in practice, we cannot say that a causal relationship exists between them. And even if same-race adoption by blacks could be shown to further cultural pluralism, there is no guarantee that cultural pluralism would challenge racism. Recall from Chapter 3 that an explicit principle of antiracism is necessary for positive social interaction and education among racial groups.

Using cultural pluralism to promote black same-race adoption treats black children as the means to furthering adult conceptions of a black cultural community. This symbolic manipulation violates the idea that black children should navigate their own racial self-identification and cultural practices as they grow up. While the goal of placing more black children in adoptive homes, regardless of racial makeup, certainly furthers the individual welfare of children, thus contributing to social welfare more generally, exempting blacks from racial randomization can only be defended by drawing a causal arrow from racial ascription to cultural practice.

Granted, Banks's policy of strict nonaccommodation would not force black prospective adopters to choose black children. Under strict nonaccommodation, blacks would be free to adopt nonblack children. Banks is confident, however, that most blacks will want to adopt black children when given the opportunity. Are the same-race preferences of black adopters less pernicious than the same-race preferences of white adopters? One could argue that the relatively small number of black adopters and the high number of black children awaiting adoption means that black adopters' preferences for black children are not likely to deprive a white child of an adoptive home. By contrast, when whites avoid adopting a black child, opting to wait for a white child or pursue independent adoption, they effectively deprive a black child of an adoptive home.

Without question, numbers matter. The overarching goal of finding adoptive homes for as many adoptable children as possible should be at the heart of adoption policy and practice. But children's welfare requires more than just finding them homes. Adoption policy and those who implement policy should also be concerned with decreasing aversive racism by encouraging TRA that flows in all directions. Blacks should be encouraged to adopt white children, not only because TRA benefits the members of their own adoptive family, but also to show others that blacks can successfully parent white children. Some might question black parents' ability to teach a white child how to be white. But if such instruction entails instilling a false sense of racial superiority in a child who happens to be born with a white skin, then it is a lesson best left untaught. The racial fissure between a white child and her black adoptive parents is likely to prompt critical reflection on the social meaning of whiteness that would otherwise not occur.

IMAGINING COMPREHENSIVE CHANGE

Banks's limited policy of strict nonaccommodation does not strike hard enough against the perpetuation of race-based social aversion via adoption. His policy prescription is not likely to affect the majority of prospective adopters in today's growing trend toward independent adoption, where adoption brokers and lawyers have supplanted agencies as key adoption intermediaries. The kind of public agency–mediated adoptions that would be subject to Banks's policy of strict nonaccommodation account for a small percentage of adoptions. Increasingly, brokers and lawyers arrange and help to formalize independent adoptions. These independent adoption intermediaries would be unaffected by Banks's antidiscrimination policy, which only applies to public adoption agencies. So even if Banks were to include prospective black adopters in strict nonaccomodation, the policy's effect would be limited to those adopting through public agencies. Independent adoptions also fall outside the jurisdiction of MEPA, the federal law banning federally funded adoption agencies from formally using race in placement decisions.

Independent adoption has grown in step with a booming economic market in reproductive technology. Market efficiency depends on the satisfaction of consumer demand, and this consumerlike attitude has seeped into the adoption world, as couples and individuals pay hefty sums to "shop" for children with specific characteristics. Margaret Jane Radin warns that "market rhetoric could create a commodified self-conception in everyone, as the result of commodifying every attribute that differentiates us and that other people value in us, and could destroy personhood as we know it."[16] To guard against this threat, Radin urges us to take a position of market inalienability, by which she means that human reproductive tissue and other aspects of our personhood may be separated from us but not traded for money. Although today's adoption system is not an explicit economic market, the ability of adopters to choose children according to racial classification and other attributes does encourage a consumerlike mindset that few question. The thought experiment of racial randomization brings this underlying consumerism to the fore. If we agree that consumerism is misapplied in adoption, what can be done to address this problem?

Mary Lyndon Shanley does not express an opinion on racial randomization, but she supports the proposition that adoption is best conceived as a publicly mediated event free of consumerism:

Placing a public agency between the original family and the adoptive family reflects the notion that the original family entrusts the child to the public (to the state as parens patriae) and that the public (in the form of the agency and its rules) accepts responsibility for the welfare of the child. Another family then assumes specific responsibility for the welfare of the child.[17]

A civic-minded approach to adoption would, in my opinion, reject consumer-like racial preferences for children. The privatization of adoption opens the door for prospective adopters—those who are wealthy enough to afford high broker and attorney fees—to discriminate on the basis of many descriptors, including race, because lawyers are committed to fulfilling the wishes of their clients, the adopters.[18] Unlike the social workers who facilitate agency adoptions, private lawyers have no stated professional responsibility to furthering social welfare.

Americans often turn to the law, and the Constitution in particular, to resolve individual conflicts and social problems. But is law the best vehicle for addressing racial discrimination in adoption? Equal-protection law has been a powerful tool, both strategically and symbolically, for those who feel socially excluded and stigmatized because of race. But civil rights law cannot force people of different races to live together in families. To accomplish broader social change that includes altering the social norm of racial homogeneity within families, we need a broad-based principle of nondiscrimination that goes beyond legal claims. The thought experiment of racial randomization is based on the constitutional principle of equal-protection law: A state must not treat citizens differently based on their racial classification unless it has a compelling reason for doing so—one that is narrowly tailored to accomplish a legitimate governmental purpose. I draw on equal-protection law not because I think that racial randomization should be implemented as policy, but because this legal definition of equal protection resonates with our moral intuitions about racial justice. This intuition tells us that black children should not be denied an adoptive home based on their racial ascription. But the thought experiment of racial randomization does not stop there. It pushes us to imagine nondiscrimination as a comprehensive moral principle applied to all aspects and stages of adoption.

OBJECTIONS TO RACIAL RANDOMIZATION

Again, racial randomization is not meant as a blueprint for crafting actual adoption policy. The thought experiment aims instead to challenge the social norm of same-race family structure, which is often transferred to adoption policy and practice. Racial classification, on its own, is not a morally justifiable basis for building a family, biological or adoptive. Race-based social aversion is a heavy obstacle, but it is by no means immovable. I now turn to some of the strongest objections to racial randomization—objections that can excavate some of our ingrained assumptions about the role that race should play in family life. Once we have a more accurate picture of our racial hopes, fears, and expectations in imagining "the family," we will be better equipped to think about how we can achieve racial justice in this unique arena of social life.

There are two major objections to the hypothetical of racial randomization. There are probably more, but I think these two lines of inquiry will cover most of the terrain. First, those who are infertile, unable, or unwilling to engage in traditional biological reproduction may object that they are being unfairly singled out as guinea pigs in a social experiment. Second, and related to the first objection, is the claim that racial randomization violates the constitutional privacy rights of prospective adopters to decide the makeup of their families. Should the constitutional ideas of freedom of association and procreative liberty be interpreted to protect the right of adopters to choose children according to racial classification?

Fairness

Individuals wishing to adopt may charge that racial randomization unfairly discriminates against those who are infertile or otherwise cannot or will not engage in coital reproduction because they are gay, lesbian, or single. One might defend race-based adoptive choice as a compensatory liberty that allows such persons to achieve the semblance of a biologically based family. If fertile heterosexual individuals are allowed to determine the racial composition of their families through the selection of a heterosexual partner, then fairness would seem to require that infertile individuals be afforded the same leeway in their family planning.

Fertile heterosexual couples are apt to exercise morally suspect private racial preferences in their reproductive decision-making calculus. In the interest of fairness, perhaps all opportunities to exercise private racial discrimination in reproductive choices ought to be hypothetically banned. This objection from fairness merits attention, especially because "private" racial choices in adoption are interlaced with commonly held assumptions about the proper role that racial classification should play in adult sexual relationships. The race of the person one chooses for a heterosexual romantic partnership is a good, albeit imperfect, predictor of the racial classification of the biological children one might bear.[19] Biologism—the attempt to imitate biological parenting—seeks to transfer this parenting expectation to the adoption context. So, from the position of biologism, the exercise of private racial choice in adoption is perceived as "natural" and "normal."

Interracial dating and marriage continue to elicit social disapproval. In 1980 black-white interracial marriages accounted for .3 percent of all marriages. By 1999 this figure had increased to .5 percent.[20] A 1992 *Boston Globe* poll found that only 73 percent of whites and 52 percent of blacks perceived interracial dating as an option.[21] Future biological parents often make racially risk-averse, consumerlike choices with respect to their children vis-à-vis their selection of a sexual partner. By racial risk-aversion, I mean those decisions based on avoiding the social costs of familial and peer-group disapproval, which is still a likely consequence of interracial romance. Maureen Reddy calls this disapproval a presumption of pathology. As a white woman married to a black man, she explains the term in the following way:

> Portrayed mostly from the outside by both black and white observers, we find our relationships treated as sick manifestations of deep-seated racial myths or rebellions against our families, background, cultures: the black partner in flight from blackness, a victim of internalized racism and white supremacism; the white partner is running from banality, in search of the exotic. These stereotypes are so ingrained in all of us in the United States that, for *both* blacks and whites, there is an automatic presumption of underlying pathology in interracial relationships. To most liberal outsiders, such relationships make a retrogressive political statement, while to conservatives, they represent an alarming, sick-by-definition result of integration.[22]

This presumption of pathology is especially palpable in perceptions of white–black interracial dating and marriage, and by extension white–black interracial families.

Race-based social aversion in the cultivation of romantic partnerships may simply be an expression of racial differentiation, not invidious racial discrimination. Does the person placing a personal advertisement in a magazine or newspaper engage in benign or invidious racial discrimination when he or she lists race as a criterion for a date? We cannot know for certain whether that racial preference stems from racism or idiosyncratic desire. It is nonetheless likely that in a race-conscious society like ours, the persistence of both social and economic racial stratification, coupled with negative racial stereotypes, will at least contribute to race-based social aversion in dating and beyond.

Parenting expectations stemming from private racial choices in dating emerge in adoption agency practice. Perhaps the most indicting evidence lies in the underreported fact that most domestic white–black adoptions have involved white adults and biracial infants—children with one original parent who self-identifies as black and one original parent who self-identifies as white. And in some cases, children who have two biological parents who self-identify as black but happen to look biracial are placed in white adoptive homes at higher rates than children with "black" phenotypes. These adoption practices underscore the intense drive toward biologism in adoption, for "these biracial children can be seen as at least a partial racial match with their white adoptive parents."[23] Under MEPA, it would be illegal for social workers at federally funded agencies to use race in such a routine and decisive way.

Maybe racial randomization should be expanded to include other social categories such as sex, ethnicity, physical ability, and religion, as these classifications are often the basis for invidious discrimination, too. Each of these social designations deserves ethical investigation. If, for example, adopters are more likely to select girls than boys, and this has the detrimental effect of longer waiting periods for boys than girls, then imagining sex-based randomization may illuminate the need to make adoption more sexually just. Issues of sexual justice in adoption are not far-fetched. Microsort, a trademarked medical technology, allows pregnant women and their partners to determine the sex of their fetuses; it is overwhelmingly being used in clinical trials to select for female babies.[24]

Other categories like physical and developmental ability pose moral and practical questions about a prospective adopter's capacity to deal with the special care needs and financial cost of raising such children. Is it morally permissible to avoid adopting a blind child? A child with Down's syndrome? Is religion a meaningful label for an infant, and thus an acceptable basis for requesting a Jewish or Christian baby? Racial randomization stirs these and other questions but does not answer them. Ethical concerns about classifying adoptable children based on other social categories call for an assessment of the consequences that a particular sorting mechanism is likely to have on children in need of adoption. While randomization may be used to evaluate the morality of using other social identifications as the basis for adoption decision-making, it is important to remember that randomization is not intended for implementation.

Should the hypothetical of racial randomization be stretched to critically evaluate biological reproductive decisions? I would extend racial randomization to reproductive decisions in the market for new reproductive technologies, because like adoption, these processes necessitate third-party mediation. When a person buys human sperm or ova for in vitro fertilization or assisted insemination, he or she enters a public, or at least less private, domain. Nonassisted biological reproduction does not typically involve a mediator. Even though such decisions are motivated by social norms that have public consequences, coital reproduction is mostly a private matter. One could argue that dating services and matchmakers act as third-party mediators in bringing heterosexual men and women together. But these mediators are not directly involved in orchestrating procreation. Randomizing coital reproduction would infringe too much on individual privacy.

Adoption is rightly distinguished from nonassisted biological reproduction. Adoptions require state coordination of the interests of those in "the adoptive triangle." Unlike adults, children lack the maturity to articulate their interests in the political arena. Hence social workers and courts must discern and promote the interests of children in need of adoption. Government has a special interest in regulating how racial classification affects children awaiting adoption because children are constitutional persons. And government also has a legitimate interest in discouraging the racial classification of human gametes because of the potential for such race-based economic transactions to revive discredited notions of discrete biological races.

While racial randomization can help us to imagine a racially just adoption system, its practical implementation would likely discourage many potential adopters from adopting altogether. The likelihood of large-scale defection is a sufficient reason not to treat racial randomization, even in a moderated form, as a policy prescription. But this practical difficulty should not deter further investigation into the morality of race-based adoptive choice. Indeed, the impracticality of racial randomization tells us something about the limits of racial integration. Racially randomized adoption pushes colorblindness to its logical conclusion. If Americans are truly committed to colorblindness, as both a legal and moral principle, then why would so many refuse to submit to a colorblind process that may land them in an interracial adoptive family?

Privacy

Linked to the objection that racial randomization discriminates against infertile persons and others who are outside nonassisted biological reproduction is the objection that prospective adopters, regardless of their reproductive ability, should be free to choose affective ties within the sphere of family life without state interference. This is an argument about privacy and family decisions. And as much as this claim is couched in the socially and religiously conservative rhetoric of "family values," it also harbors a subtext of consumerism. Although the privacy objection to my thought experiment is more powerful than the objection based in fairness, it can be refuted on the grounds that it also fails to properly distinguish adoptive families from biological families.

There is a strong presumption in the United States that adoption is a private act, analogous to the private act of procreation. "Privacy" refers to associative freedom—a freedom that encompasses the freedom to form social bonds with some persons and not others based on a wide range of criteria. If adoption is like biological reproduction in the sense that individuals have the freedom to choose a sexual partner according to any number of personal prejudices, then does it follow that prospective adopters may be equally choosy in their selection of an adoptive child?

Few people question the morality of this discrimination because U.S. constitutional doctrine has maintained that individual acts of racial discrimination, unsupported by government, are beyond the reach of the Fourteenth Amendment. Reva Siegel, discussing affirmative action jurisprudence, shows that the right to privately discriminate on the basis of race has taken on different rhetorical forms since the first judicial constructions of the Fourteenth Amendment. While opponents of civil rights legislation have appealed to associational liberty as a rationale for private racial discrimination since Reconstruction, Siegel observes that "racial discourses of the private are now more commonly couched in a related, but distinct, market idiom that emphasizes individual and/or group competition."[25] In this market idiom, the racial discriminations of adopters become private economic decisions.[26]

Treating the family as categorically private is neither accurate nor desirable. As many feminist scholars have pointed out, the division that sets family units apart from government intervention can, and all too often does, facilitate the domestic subordination of women and children.[27] Moreover, families have never been free of government intervention. From the start, the state issues marriage licenses and alters one's tax status. Parents are legally obligated to provide their children a formal education, either by sending them to an accredited school or providing a state-approved curriculum at home. There are nonetheless many private choices generally associated with family life that we cherish. Chief among these is the freedom to choose with whom one will make a home and create a family. These "fundamental values" are often discussed under the constitutional rubric of freedom of association and procreative liberty.

The Supreme Court has interpreted the Fourteenth Amendment's due-process clause as containing a right to privacy and the First Amendment as containing a right to associative freedom for the purpose of expression. This theory of constitutional interpretation—alternatively referred to as noninterpretivism and nonoriginalism—holds that "courts should go beyond [the explicit or "clearly implicit" text of the Constitution] and enforce norms that cannot be discovered within the four corners of the document."[28] The doctrinal concepts of both associative freedom and procreative freedom exemplify noninterpretivism, as neither is explicitly mentioned in the Constitution. Noninterpretivism can be traced back to the Court's landmark ruling in the 1905 case *Lochner v. New York* that the due-process clause prohibits the regulation of working hours for bakers, thus establishing a constitutional "liberty of contract" based extratextually on the Fourteenth Amendment.[29] So-called substantive due-process adjudication reached its height in the 1973 *Roe v. Wade* decision, in which the Court held that the Fourteenth Amendment's due-process clause contains a right to privacy broad enough to support a woman's right to procure an abortion during the first trimester of pregnancy without state interference.[30]

The noninterpretivist notions of associative and procreative freedom were most intertwined in the 1965 case *Griswold v. Connecticut*, which struck down a Connecticut statute banning the use of contraceptives by married couples.[31] The majority held that "zones of privacy" emanated from "penumbras" found in the First, Third, Fourth, Fifth, and Ninth amendments. *Griswold* leaned heavily on the assertion that marriage is an inviolable zone of privacy. Writing for the Court, Justice William O. Douglas issued a powerful declaration:

We deal with a right of privacy older than the Bill of Rights—older than our political parties, older than our school system. Marriage is a coming together for better or for worse, hopefully enduring, and intimate to the degree of being sacred. It is an association that promotes a way of life, not causes; a harmony in living, not political faiths; a bilateral loyalty, not commercial or social projects. Yet it is an association for as noble a purpose as any involved in our prior decisions.[32]

More specifically, Douglas argues that a married couple's sexual relationship is well beyond legislative scope; it is "sacred." At the heart of the majority's opinion, as well as Arthur J. Goldberg and William J. Brennan's concurrence, is visceral outrage at the prospect of police access to "marital bedrooms." That idea, Douglas writes, "is repulsive to the notions of privacy surrounding the marriage relationship." There are real dangers associated with shielding domestic relationships from state intervention, to which I alluded earlier, such as domestic violence and unjust divisions of labor. Although outside the present analysis, these concerns are worth keeping in mind.

The relevant question to be derived from the *Griswold* decision is "Do these constitutionally based arguments for associative and procreative freedom sustain the objection that adopters should be permitted to assert racial preferences in the adoption placement process?" My answer turns on a prior question: "Is adoption analogous to procreation?" According to biologism, the answer is yes. The strongest claim in support of biologism is that it downplays the "genetic strangeness" of the adopted child, thus arguably reducing the social stigma that many adopted individuals feel. Likewise, adoptive parents may choose same-race children to avoid the stigma of being identified by others as infertile—a label often associated with personal failure. They may also wish to avoid strangers' rude stares and invasive questioning that racially heterogeneous families encounter. One stigma often associated with TRA is the perception of an interracial sexual relationship. Patricia Irwin Johnston, a white adoptive mother of an African American and Hispanic daughter, comments: "We were shocked to find that when one parent went out with baby, reactions from both black and white people were cold and standoffish. There was a definite unspoken criticism, which we finally came to understand came from the assumption that they were observing an adult involved in a transracial sexual relationship."[33] Social stigma and prejudice are not, however, good reasons for analogizing adoption to procreation. Instead of molding adoptive families to fit the contours of societal prejudice, a thought experiment of racial randomization questions our prior assumptions about race and familial belonging.

An explicit acknowledgment of the nonbiological nature of adoption produces individual and social goods. One of the goods that can result from imagining randomized placement is a constraint on the kind of selfishness that accompanies the seemingly "natural" desire to reproduce oneself or one's partner. Many people harbor some desire to see a "miniature likeness of me" in a child of "my own." Yet this drive does not mean that we are justified in transferring this selfishness to the realm of adoption, and basing our notion of adoptive parenting on biological parenting. Biologism is after all the reason we tend to think of adoption as abnormal, unnatural, and "a choice of last resort."[34]

To have choices suggests some measure of control. Choosing an already born child, rather than giving birth to a child, suggests that prospective adoptive parents can exercise control precisely where "nature"/biology would have held the reins. We may wish for our biological children to resemble us physically, to pursue careers similar to our own, and to share our opinions and outlook. But we also know that recessive genes may render such biological offspring physically dissimilar to both parents, and that biological children are apt to pursue activities and careers divergent from those of their parents. When gaps such as these occur, a common quip is "I must have been adopted!"

The desire to have the apple fall near to the tree may be an inescapable component of our being. But again, the mere presence of the desire is not an adequate justification for its implementation in adoption. There are larger questions of social justice to consider—questions that may require us not to put our biologism into practice. The larger social concern motivating this book is the vexing matter of racial justice in the United States. Unrestrained consumer choice in adoption holds tremendous potential for publicly reinforcing racist private choices about what a proper family looks like.

While our intuitions about justice are tied to constitutionalism, we cannot rely solely on constitutional arguments to fight racism. As shown in Chapter 2, constitutional jurisprudence sanctions private racial discrimination. We may be able to draw a legal distinction between private and public racism, but the picture becomes less clear when we attempt to delineate morally between these two domains.

Private racial discrimination in the construction of family life, biological and adoptive, comports with the status quo and thus fails to raise an eyebrow. We think it normal and uninteresting when a white heterosexual couple adopts a healthy white infant. Yet when a white couple adopts a black child, curiosity abounds: "a crazy kind of look from people in a passing car, or a little extra room around our blankets at the beach."[35] The thought experiment of racial randomization aims to catalyze a rethinking of status quo assumptions about which persons "belong together" in families. De facto racial segregation in the social construction of family life is an early temporal point in the re-ignition of our structural racism. Antiracist intervention at the point of adoptive placement is a necessary, albeit small, part of a larger project of discouraging intergenerational racism.

CHAPTER 5

Navigating the Involuntary Association of TRA

Political deliberation over TRA should include a broad-based principle of nondiscrimination that goes beyond equal-protection law. The purpose of the racial randomization hypothetical was to draw our attention to race-based adopter choice, which is typically ignored by colorblind arguments in favor of TRA. My goal is not to make race-based adopter choice illegal, but to prod adopters to stop this form of racial discrimination without legal threat. This chapter combines the moral principle of nondiscrimination with the idea of racial navigation to theoretically explore "life after randomization." Although racial randomization does not automatically lead to racial navigation, the two concepts compliment each other. Together, they establish the theoretical basis for a race-conscious defense of TRA. Moral inquiry into the use of race in adoption should reach beyond the moment of adoptive placement to envision adoption as a unique, lifelong family tie. All children are potential adults who possess the ability to navigate the involuntary associations of both race and family.

The practical need for flexible racial self-identification is made explicit in TRA, as children are forced to integrate the racial difference between themselves and their adoptive family. This racial schism, plus the absence of a genetic tie, upsets the conventional wisdom that racial self-identification ought to be acquired wholesale from a genetically tethered family. Two theoretical concepts factor into this enterprise of racial navigation: individual agency and involuntary racial association. My theory of racial navigation strives to maximize individual agency in identity formation while simultaneously recognizing the practical constraints of racial categories. The goal is to complicate rather than simplify the experience of racial self-identification.

Submission to racial imposition is a kind of self-defeat. The language of defeat may seem hyperbolic. After all, it is possible that the failure to develop a creative, or even active, self-identification signals nothing more than a failure of the imagination. Not everyone can be, or desires to be, creative with respect to the elusive and daunting concept of "the self." Embedded in this skepticism is concern about the elitism that such a call to creativity might evoke. Keeping this worry in mind, I show that a particular variant of racial self-fashioning need not be an elitist aspiration. On the contrary, this mode of racial self-identification is accessible to everyone and is democratically grounded.

I explore the concept of involuntary association as it relates to the concepts of race and family. Racial categories constitute an involuntary association that must figure into the self-concepts of those identified by others as having a race. Adopted individuals have a dual familial involuntary association: original and adoptive. Both families, whether physically present or not, affect an adopted person's sense of self. In TRA, the racial disjuncture between these family associations must be navigated. The path of navigation will vary from person to person. Orlando Patterson's metaphor of natal alienation illuminates the inevitable loss that accompanies all adoptions. I then consider two alternative normative theories of racial self: cosmopolitanism, as presented by Jeremy Waldron and K. Anthony Appiah, and racial solidity, as articulated by Molefi Kete Asante. Racial navigation occupies a middle ground between these two models of racial self-identification.

RACIAL INVOLUNTARY ASSOCIATION

Passive racial self-identification means uncritical absorption of racial ascription. The involuntary association of racial classification describes a series of brute facts about our existence, but our individual identities should not be frozen by such facts. In *Anti-Semite and Jew,* Jean-Paul Sartre argues that self-identification is constructed and reconstructed through interpersonal engagement.[1] Infusing his theory of existentialism with a Marxist twist, Sartre posited that social identifications would change over time in a dialectical process that culminated in a world swept clean of social categories, including race. Without social categories like black and white, racial self-identification would be meaningless. He recommended temporary multicul-turalism en route to no-culturalism, in the same way that Karl Marx called for class-consciousness as a precondition to achieving a class-less society. For Sartre, racial identities and their associated cultural practices are the products of existential engagement rather than of essence. On this, Sartre was absolutely right. Jewishness, like black-ness, is a reaction to an imposition from without. Black self-identifica-tion is a response to racism in its myriad forms. The anti-Semite, like the racist, relegates certain people to a category deemed inferior to her own self-understanding, thus creating a sense of false superiority.

Sartre's theory of identity construction is compelling, but I am not convinced that racial self-identification can or should wither away. Racial categories are rooted in racism, but racism does not capture the full meaning that racial categories hold for individuals. Evelyn Brooks Higginbotham underscores this point: "Racial meanings were never internalized by blacks and whites in an identical way. The language of race has historically been what Bakhtin calls a double-voiced dis-course—serving the voice of black oppression and the voice of black liberation."[2] Responding to racial classification can be a liberating ex-perience of subverting racial meanings, maintaining personal distance from racial stereotypes, and personalizing one's blackness. We have the potential to participate in what Michael Walzer calls "constructive activity." He writes, "These [different historical cultures] have an inner strength that Sartre never acknowledges, and the people they sustain, who also sustain them, are not yet candidates for disappear-ance."[3] In emphasizing this positive aspect of identity development, Walzer attributes an "inner strength" to what he terms historical cul-tures. This imbues historical cultures with an almost mythical quality, making the idea of racial self-identification susceptible to solidifica-tion. Racial navigation is meant to resist ossification, as well as the tendency to treat racial self-identification as strictly negative.

Walzer's critique exposes the assimilation imperative lurking be-hind Sartre's description of an identityless society. The final result of Sartre's historical determinism is a society in which all minority groups have subordinated their particularity to the dominant set of cultural norms: "After all, what would men and women be like after the end of social pluralism? Perhaps Sartre believes that they will be simply and universally human. In fact, as the whole argument of his book suggests, they will surely be French."[4] Transporting Sartre's paradigm to the United States is likely to produce a "raceless" world in which a white middle-class American identity and its attendant cultural norms prevail.

In *Black Orpheus*, Sartre addresses the existential reality of racial involuntary association more directly.[5] The Paris intellectual scene of the 1940s and 1950s was being rocked by a group of young black Francophone intellectuals. Their political and intellectual movement was a manifestation of black cultural nationalism dubbed Négritude. In its most basic form, Négritude turned existentialism on its head, positing that essence precedes existence, or more precisely that African essence precedes colonial existence. For instance, Léopold Sédar Senghor, who would become the first president of independent Senegal, asserted that blacks throughout the African diaspora maintained an African spiritual, emotional, and psychic essence regardless of their geographical location or "race-mixing." Blacks in the United States were no exception: "What strikes me about the Negroes in America is the permanence not of the physical but of the psychic characteristics of the Negro-African, despite race-mixing, despite the new environment."[6]

Proclaiming an African essence, the proponents of Négritude were determined to construct a counternarrative to colonial racism. Sartre endorsed the antiracist motivation behind Négritude, but he parted company with scholar-activists such as Senghor and Aimé Césaire over the matter of Négritude's ambitions. Whereas Senghor and Césaire asserted the permanence of African essence, Sartre maintained that Négritude constituted the antiracist antithesis to the thesis of colonial racism. Eventually, this dialectical struggle would produce the synthesis of a raceless world—a world in which the notion of race would carry no existential meaning. In Sartre's view, "Négritude, as liberty, is the basic concept and the point of departure; the task is to cause it to pass from the immediate to the mediate, to develop its theme. It is thus for the black to die of the white world to be reborn of the black soul, as the platonic philosopher dies of the body to be reborn of the truth."[7] With this formula, Sartre tried to preserve the integrity of his existentialism. Existence still preceded essence.

With Sartre, I reject the idea of racial essence. But I leave Sartre at the moment he imagines a raceless future. Even if a raceless world were possible, abolishing racial categories is not necessary for achieving a strong sense of personal agency in shaping one's life. Sartre's colorblind vision fails to take seriously the proposition that the colonial encounter and Middle Passage have indelibly marked human existence with racial categories. K. Anthony Appiah's argument that these historical experiences require African writers to ask a different existential question from their European counterparts applies to African Americans, too. Appiah argues that although "the European may feel that the problem of who he or she is can be a private problem, the African asks always not 'who am I?' but 'who are we?' and 'my' problem is not mine alone but 'ours.'"[8]

FAMILIAL INVOLUNTARY ASSOCIATION

The question "Who are we?" is generated by involuntary racial association. Families are the first involuntary association we experience. And it is here that the identity "conversation" must begin. In Walzer's words, "The first constraint is familial and social in character. We are born members of a kin group, and of a nation or country, and of a social class—and these three together go a long way toward determining the people with whom we associate for the rest of our lives (even if we hate our relatives, think patriotism sentimental, never attain class consciousness)."[9] Although Walzer does not mention race in this list of involuntary associations, we can assume that the seeds of racial identity take root in what Walzer terms a "kin group," or family. We are born into a race in the sense of being subjected to an identity conversation with intimate others in a family setting that is personal and social. We also develop our sense of self through dialogue with intimate others and strangers both near and far.

For better or worse, one's family, whatever its configuration, is the first "school," the first institution of socialization. As such, families stand as critical transfer points for the intergenerational perpetuation of racial meanings. We think of race as a solidifying force because we live with a social presumption that one receives one's racial identity from one's family—specifically, one's parents. Biological same-race family structure is normative. Most American children *are* raised by biological parents who share their racial classification, but that social norm is neither inevitable nor optimal. Interracial biological parenting of biracial or multiracial children wavers from this social norm, yet monoracial biological family structure still has a firm grip on our social ontology.

Transracial adoption disturbs the model of genetically based family ties and breaks the presumption of intergenerational racial continuity. Adopters volunteer to parent children who, no matter how young they are at the time of adoption, have already been born into an involuntary association: their families of origin. Hence adopted children are connected to their original and adoptive families. Acknowledging this double family knot does not mean that adoptive families are inferior to biological families. On the contrary, TRA sparks theoretical insight into racial self-reflection. While the need for racial navigation is made more explicit in the case of TRA, its critical posture toward racial self-identification is a universal good.

The portability of this model is evident in the autobiographical documentary film *Secret Daughter*, written and produced by June Cross. Cross, the daughter of a white woman and a black man, recounts the story of how she became a "secret" in her white mother's life, and how she began tearing down that pretense as an adult filmmaker.[10] At the age of four, Cross was sent to live with a black family in Atlantic City, New Jersey, to protect the career of her mother's new husband, white television star Larry Storch. The film details her personal efforts to create a sense of self in response to the imposition of racial classification, both within and without the intimate setting of her family. In a painfully ironic twist, a 1966 Hollywood publicity photo identifies Cross as the adopted daughter of her white mother and white stepfather. Through a series of interviews with both original and "adoptive" relatives (Cross was not formally adopted by the black family who raised her), Cross peels back multiple layers of her life, navigating the idea of race in her quest for self-understanding. She confronts the social fact of race but does not permit that reality to overwhelm her sense of self. Instead of caving in to the force of racial imposition, Cross paints a complex portrait of herself as a black woman. The following exchange between Cross and a member of her black "adoptive" family illustrates racial navigation:

AUNT SHEILA: How could you not feel fury and anger toward her about the position that she put you in? She turned you over to somebody else.

JUNE: That's a mother–daughter issue, though. That has nothing to do with race.

AUNT SHEILA: Well, in this case it has something to do with race, because that was why it happened.

JUNE: Yeah, but my brother also got turned over, and he was white.

AUNT SHEILA: But she could say, "This is my son," and did say, "This is my son." She didn't feel she could and she did not with you.

JUNE: I think what I felt—I do feel a sense of abandonment, but on a mother–daughter level, not a black–white level.[11]

Cross challenges Sheila's racial reductionism. It's not that race plays no part in Cross's understanding of her mother's decision to send her away; it's that her sense of abandonment is also about a mother–daughter relationship. Her identity as a black woman is shaped by many family ties that involve, but are not defined solely by, racial fissure. Cross contemplates her white mother and stepfather, a white brother who was also "sent away," the absence of her black father, and her connection to the black family who raised her. All of these relationships affect Cross's self-concept, and their integration requires a willingness to examine and revise one's sense of self over time. *Secret Daughter* shows that family bonds—genetic, adoptive, and chosen—influence personal racial meanings and vice versa. Racial identity should not be thought of as something that individuals simply acquire from parents. Instead, we should examine and revise our self-concepts through conversation and dialogue with a wide range of people over our lifetimes.

NATAL ALIENATION

Adopted children arrive in their adoptive homes with a prior set of family ties, a prior involuntary association. Even when children are adopted within the first year of their lives—as most are, because adopters generally want to be able to celebrate their child's first birthday—they have already had the experience of being born into a plethora of particularity that, if not for biologism (the desire to imitate a biological family), we would regard as relevant to the development of an individual's life script.[12]

When a black child is adopted by a white family or a white child is adopted by a black family, the racial "root" of the first dimension will affect the adopted person's self-concept in some way. Transracially adopted individuals will need the "reference point" of their original family to make sense of the way in which others in the society perceive them. This does not mean that original family members must be physically present in an adopted person's life, or even personally known to the adoptee. The reference point can simply be the knowledge that some or all of one's original family shares at least part of one's racial designation. Note the distinction here between racial classification and racial self-identification. I am not saying that adopted children *get* their racial self-identification from their original parents.

Whether original parents are known to the adopted person or not, natal alienation is a part of all adoptions. Children are physically transferred from their original families to adoptive families, and parental rights are legally transferred to adoptive parents, placing a legal imprimatur on this alienation. Legal eradication, or invalidation, of the original family tie does not guarantee a clean break. The first involuntary association of the child's original family marks the child's existential starting point. We cannot deny this aspect of adoption. Orlando Patterson uses the term *natal alienation* to describe an aspect of all slavery. Slavery is by no means an apt metaphor for adoption. Still, it is worth noting with Patterson that natal alienation always involves emotional distress. The slave, Patterson writes, "was truly a genealogical isolate. . . . He had a past, to be sure. But a past is not a heritage. Everything has a history, including sticks and stones. Slaves differed from other human beings in that they were not allowed freely to integrate the experience of their ancestors into their lives, to inform their understanding of social reality with the inherited meanings of their natural forebears, or to anchor the living present in any conscious community of memory."[13] Some opponents of TRA have misappropriated the metaphor of slavery to draw attention to macro concerns of structural racism. For example, Ruth-Arlene Howe writes, "Like the slave trader/merchants of Gorée Island who worked to meet a market demand for free slave labor, these professional TRA proponents seek to secure a steady supply of infants to satisfy a demand."[14] Such hyperbole is not conducive to a rational discussion of the effects of racism in the adoption system. Natal alienation does, however, bring some of the harder realities of adoption into focus. Biologism tries to will the first familial association, the original family, into nonexistence. Or at least biologism seeks to minimize the effect of the original family on the adopted child's life. Rather than treating the original family as if it were an impediment, we ought to treat this first familial association as an integral part of an adopted person's identity journey.

Sartre says nothing about family ties and their impact on racial existence. He believed that racism, as he witnessed it in France and in French colonial Africa, imprisoned blacks in a social category that would fade with time. He added that "black" skin color made blackness more constricting than Jewishness: "A Jew, white among white men, can deny that he is a Jew, can declare himself a man among men. The Negro cannot deny that he is a Negro nor claim for himself this abstract uncolored humanity. He is black. Thus he is held to authenticity."[15] Race will someday wither away, according to Sartre, but the person identified by others as black is black in the here and now and must deal with that existential reality. As with all people living in racial categories, this racial existence holds for black individuals who grow up in white adoptive homes.

The following testimony given by a biracial woman raised by white adoptive parents demonstrates the use of a racial referent, even when the reference is not directly to original family members. Recounting her friendship with another biracial adoptee, she writes, "What I remember most poignantly from Kai's and my college days are the frequent journeys we made on the Metro-North trains to Manhattan. Twenty minutes to 125th Street! We rode those trains at dawn, returning from a night of clubbing, or in the late afternoon after freshman seminar, on schedule with the domestic workers and other laborers traveling between Westchester and the Bronx and Harlem. I would survey each Black face, for some resemblance to my own."[16] The search for a black face that resembles "my own" is part of the search to understand oneself as belonging to a racial category. Applying K. Anthony Appiah's formulation to the situation of Arican Americans, the author's private question of "Who am I?" is unavoidably linked to the public activity of surveying black faces on a commuter train, asking, "Who are we?"

Does the existential value of racial reference support an argument for open adoption, which maintains some degree of communication between the original parents (usually only the original mother is involved) and the adopting family? Open adoption is one way of providing identity reference points for an adopted person, but it is not the only way of encouraging racial navigation. Adoptees should have as much access to information about their original families as they grow up as is practically and prudently possible. In some cases, closed adoptions are necessary because the original parents are unfit or show no interest in being involved in the child's life. Whether and to what degree contact between the original parents and the adoptive parents should be encouraged will depend on the particular case. In any event, adopted individuals should be given access to nonidentifying information about their original parents as a way of encouraging racial navigation. All adoptions involve natal alienation, and thus pain. Transracial adoptions involve an added dimension of racial natal alienation. But the pain experienced by all three parties in the adoption triad is not inconsolable. And while adoption is about loss, it is also about adding new dimensions to one's life.

Ultimately, we must reconcile our freedom with others, but we can still develop a strong sense of individuality under the practical constraint of racial categories. My focus on race is not meant to deny or minimize the impact of other issues in family life such as divorce, substance abuse, domestic violence, and financial stability. Like all children, adopted children must often cope with these and other stressors. Race figures prominently, but its trials can be and often are affected by these common family problems.

BETWEEN COSMOPOLITANISM AND RACIAL SOLIDITY

Racial navigation lies somewhere between two alternative theories of the racial self: cosmopolitanism and racial solidity. Although both of these theories contribute to a process of active racial self-identification, neither provides an adequate account of active racial response. Cosmopolitanism collapses descriptions of particular life circumstances into prescriptions for the good life, whereas theories of racial solidity steamroll racial complexity.

The Cosmopolitan Project
Cosmopolitanism, as presented by Jeremy Waldron and K. Anthony Appiah, is an attractive theory of personal identity because it values

strong individual agency and creative self-imagining. Although consistent with racial navigation, cosmopolitanism presupposes certain material conditions such as wealth, education, and lack of domestic responsibilities (for instance, child care responsibilities) in staking out its normative argument for a life well lived, making cosmopolitanism vulnerable to charges of elitism. I offer racial navigation as an anti-elitist cosmopolitanism alternative.

According to the cosmopolitan story, human beings thrive in an active state of engagement with persons, places, and things that are perceived to be in a relationship of difference with who or what one imagines oneself to be. The prescription is that individuals should be open to revising parts of their self-concepts in light of these encounters. In Waldron's words, "Humans are curious and adventurous animals: they travel, they migrate, they trade, they fight, and they plunder. And they report back what they have found out about the ways in which others live (and trade and fight etc.). They bring back tales of exotic customs as well as the exotic goods they have purchased or stolen."[17]

From this snapshot of what it means to be human, Waldron argues that a long record of "human adventure" has resulted in more cultural hybridity and mélange than is usually admitted by those who describe and affirm notions of cultural distinctiveness and or purity. Cultural identification, Waldron points out, depends on perspective. Tourist Boards and elementary teachers are not likely to refer to Catholicism, wearing Levi's, and drinking Coke, as "being Guatemalan" even though most Guatemalans do those things. Identity politics chooses the view from outside, and beckons insiders to board the tourist bus, too. In other words, "to congratulate oneself on following 'the norms of my community' is already to take a point of view somewhat external to those norms, rather than to subscribe wholeheartedly to the substantive commitments that they embody."[18] Here Waldron is saying that those who take their cultural endeavors seriously will not feel the urge to brag. Nor should we misperceive cultural differences as the basis for according someone moral respect. Whereas cultural practices and identifications change, our shared humanity stays constant.

Although Waldron does not discuss racial identity in the United States, his thesis in "What is Cosmopolitan?" supports my critique of racial solidity—a non-negotiable description of blackness that is often couched in cultural specificity. Waldron argues against the sort of authenticity implied by communitarian and nationalist statements of tightly scripted identity, praising instead the script that is hybrid and open to revision. "What is Cosmpolitan?" responds to Will Kymlicka's critique of an earlier article in which Waldron had described the cosmopolitan person as a "frequent flyer"—a metaphor that Waldron now regrets.[19] "I spoke of someone who did not associate his identity with any secure sense of place, someone who did not take his cultural identity to be defined by any bounded subset of the cultural resources available in the world."[20]

The "frequent flyer" is a jet-set consumer, dipping into cultural practices without engaging cultural difference in a sustained way that would respect the view from inside. "He did not take his identity as anything definitive, as anything homogenous that might be muddied or compromised if he studied Greek, ate Chinese, wore clothes made in Korea, worshipped with the Book of Common Prayer, listened to arias by Verdi sung by a Maori diva on Japanese equipment, gave lectures in Buenos Aires, followed Israeli politics, or practiced Buddhist meditation techniques."[21] Waldron's rehabilitated "frequent flyer" may have cut down on his conspicuous consumption, but he is still likely to carry an American Express Gold Card. Missing from Waldron's cosmopolitan project is an account of how material conditions make it possible for some people to travel far beyond their home, while others stay put because of poverty and or caretaking responsibilities to children and other relatives.

Waldron does say that his conception of cosmopolitanism is not meant to give the impression that there is nothing cosmopolitan about the person who remains in one geographical location his or her entire life. According to Waldron, "a person who grows up in Manhattan, for example, cannot but be aware of a diversity of cultures, a diversity of human practices and experiences, indeed a diversity of languages clamoring for his attention. They are there on the streets, in Greenwich Village or on the Upper West Side."[22] Does this mean that the person who does not grow up in a place like Manhattan cannot participate in a cosmopolitan way of life? I suspect that Waldron would allow that non-native New Yorkers can benefit from the variety of cultural forms available on "the street." But even so, not everyone can or wishes to live in Manhattan or Bombay, London, and Paris—other cosmopolitan cities cited by Waldron. In this sense, Waldron's cosmopolitan theory lac ks democratic accessbility.

But let us revisit Waldron's characterization of the Manhattanite as cosmopolitan by location. I wish it was true, but I fear this depiction of the Manhattanite is much too sanguine. True, the Manhattanite cannot avoid encountering races, ethnicities, and cultural practices different from his or her own. But forced encounters with difference "on the streets" do not always translate into the open-mindedness that Waldron's cosmopolitan approach to lifestyle prescribes. Daily life in urban centers like New York is a crash course in racial segregation and distributive injustice. Sociologist John Logan comments, "I think New Yorkers often feel that they live in a very diverse place and that it must be very integrated. And it's true that in almost every part of New York there's at least some minority presence. But what we don't see is the extent to which the neighborhoods that have real concentrations of minority-group members really are isolated enclaves, and very large shares of those groups live in those places. We don't see those because it's not our experience, but it is the experience of the members of those groups."[23]

Perhaps Waldron is celebrating city life as potential in the way that Iris Young sees city life as a blueprint for imagining a normative ideal of social relations that affirms group difference.[24] In Young's view, city life holds theoretical promise because so many different communities live within a relatively contained geographical space. Even though neighborhoods continue to be segregated according to class, race, ethnicity, and religious beliefs, we can imagine a model in which these differences are experienced positively by city-dwellers after structural changes were effected to place them in a more just relationship with one another.[25] Young makes it clear that her normative ideal is not intended for implementation as such. Rather, she wants to alert us to the possibility of change. "Social change," she reminds us, "arises from politics, not philosophy. Ideals are a crucial step in emancipatory politics, however, because they dislodge our assumption that what is given is necessary. They offer standpoints from which to criticize the given, and the inspiration for imagining alternatives."[26]

Theoretical analyses of the politics of TRA can and should foster such imagination. Cosmopolitanism, as conceived by Waldron, offers a compelling call for embracing a plurality of social identifications and cultural practices within oneself. Yet closer scrutiny reveals that such creativity and flexibility are predicated on a narrow descriptive reality. Because travel plays such a pivotal part in cosmopolitan projects, cosmopolitan success will depend on one's ability to leave one's home. Waldron allows that one can become cosmopolitan simply by living in a cosmopolitan place like Manhattan or Bombay. But again not everyone can live or wants to live in those cities. In the end, cosmopolitanism does not deliver the democratic access it advertises.

K. Anthony Appiah tries to defend cosmopolitanism against this objection by developing the idea of "cosmopolitan patriots." Where Waldron implied that the person who did not travel or live in a cosmopolitan city was worse off, Appiah maintains that even these individuals can share in a cosmopolitan payoff:

> In a world of cosmopolitan patriots, people would accept the citizen's responsibility to nurture the culture and politics of their homes. Many would, no doubt, spend their lives in the places that shaped them; and that is one of the reasons local practices would be sustained and transmitted. But many would move, and that would mean that cultural practices would travel also (as they have always traveled). The result would be a world in which each local form of human life was the result of long term and persistent processes of cultural hybridization: a world, in that respect, much like the world we live in now.[27]

It is instructive that what Appiah ends up describing is something very close to the status quo. This point reveals cosmopolitanism's limited prescriptive value. There will always be a small number of people who travel and plunder, and they will always be able to do so precisely because there are many more people who stay put. Perhaps there is some trickle-down benefit to those unable or unwilling to travel in the form of cultural hybridization of their homes by those who do travel, but this does not dissolve the elitism driving the cosmopolitan project. The cosmopolitans have not paved a democratically accessible road to reach the attractive destinations they portray. The altered mentality of a cosmopolitan approach to lifestyle should not depend on extraordinary opportunities such as world travel or moving to New York City.

Appiah explicitly acknowledges that racism can and often does limit the ability for black Americans to imagine themselves as cosmopolitans or even cosmopolitan patriots, but he does not give racism its existential due. As discussed in chapter 1, he proposes a "banal postmodernism," imploring us to "live with fractured identities; engage in identity play; find solidarity, yes, but recognize contingency, and, above all, practice irony."[28] These prescriptions are alluring. One could not ask for more in the way of maximizing individual agency. The problem is that this agency is too abstracted from lived experiences of racism's material and psychological effects.

Appiah's "banal postmodernism" must be read in the context of his larger efforts to separate the idea of race from the idea of culture. He warns against conflating these two notions. And he is right to say that no singular African American culture exists; there is tremendous variation with respect to the cultural practices that black Americans engage in. But this does not mean that there is no such thing as African American culture. While Appiah is right to say that this culture is not biologically determined, he underestimates the degree to which the shared experience of racism in the United States has produced, and continues to produce, cultural artifacts and practices that can be described as African American. He explains his rejection of the term *African American culture* in this way:

> I have insisted that African Americans do not have a single culture, in the sense of shared language, values, practices, and meanings. But many people who think of races as groups defined by shared cultures, conceive that sharing in a different way. They understand black people as sharing black culture *by definition*: jazz or hip-hop belongs to an African American, whether she likes it or knows anything about it, because it is culturally marked as black. Jazz belongs to a person who knows nothing about it more fully or naturally than it does to a white jazzman.[29]

Black people share the experience of racism. Over time, there have been numerous responses to this constraint on human freedom. Cultural artifacts and practices deriving from historical responses to racism can be described as African American. Appiah's argument washes over this situation too quickly. It is not that the white jazzman is an inauthentic jazzman. Rather, the white jazzman is engaged in a black cultural form that is itself a mixture of African and European cultural elements. The definition of black culture does not hang on whether a particular black person has an affinity for jazz or hip-hop.

These cultural forms are part of an overarching and multifaceted story of what black Americans have done in the face of racism and its effects.

Racial Solidity

Racial categories weigh heavily on the lives of those identified as black. I have been arguing for the use of personal agency to maintain some space between one's racial self-identification and categorical racial imposition. No doubt I am calling for some tricky maneuvering, but racial navigation is possible and worthwhile. Theories of racial solidity make the mistake of conceptualizing racial classification as an overwhelming social experience. In their zeal to acknowledge racial categories as constraining, theorists like Molefi Kete Asante end up foreclosing the possibility of resisting racial acquiescence. Asante's theory of racial solidity would deny the validity of James McBride's self-description, discussed in Chapter 1. McBride, the son of a white Jewish American mother and an African American father, describes himself as a black man with something of a Jewish soul. Asante would insist that McBride misunderstands himself, and that McBride's authentic self is African, "straight up and down." Describing his own racial self-understanding, Asante states, "My identity was solid, not fluid."[30]

This method of self-understanding exemplifies the kind of non-negotiable racial identity that Waldron and Appiah oppose. In Asante's view, people who are identified as black should choose an African identity and comport this identity as solid, not fluid. "I was," Asante proclaims, "straight up and down an African in my consciousness and that fact did not contradict my nationality as an American; it simply threw everything into the most ordered reality possible for me."[31] Asante substitutes "African" for "Jew" in Sartre's psychological portrait of anti-Semitism:

> The racist anti-Africanite finds the activities of the misoriented
> African comforting for his or her anti-Africanism. The misori-
> ented African, much like Sartre's inauthentic Jew, runs away
> from his or her Africanity by attempting to deny it, conceal it, or
> attack it. Unlike the Jew, who seldom wishes to destroy his or her
> Jewishness, the misoriented African assumes that he or she is not
> African and therefore takes exception to those who remind him
> or her that she bears all of the major characteristics of resem-

blance to those who are African. Thus, the misoriented African, that is, the inauthentic African, allows the dominance of the single-consciousness of Europe to conquer him or her. At that moment, and not before, the misoriented African becomes for all practical purposes the spitting image of the racist anti-Africanite. Neither a victim of double-consciousness nor attuned to the consciousness of his or her own historical experiences, which would center the person, the misoriented African becomes disoriented and believes that he or she is actually a European.[32]

But Asante fails to note the key distinction Sartre draws between Jewishness and blackness in the matter of authenticity: "A Jew, white among white men, can deny that he is a Jew, can declare himself a man among men. The Negro cannot deny that he is a Negro nor claim for himself this abstract uncolored humanity. He is black. Thus he is held to authenticity."[33] Blackness is marked by skin pigmentation and other immutable physical characteristics and thus cannot be escaped. Asante also ignores Sartre's forecast for the elimination of racial categories altogether.

It is strange that Asante does not refer to Sartre's play *Black Orpheus,* in which he vindicates exactly the sort of black nationalist existential response expressed by Asante. Black nationalism is the redress that whites should have expected: "Insulted, enslaved, he [the Negro] redresses himself; he accepts the word 'Negro' which is hurled at him as an epithet, and revindicates himself, in pride, as black in the face of white."[34] But Sartre supported black nationalism as just one necessary stage in a dialectical struggle that would eventually sap racial categories of any social meaning. One can disagree with Sartre's vision of racelessness (or assimilation to the dominant racial group) without dismissing the potential for black nationalism to provide a temporary form of existential healing.

Retreating from racial complexity can be a reasonable way of making sense of a race-conscious world. Asante knows that African American cultural practices are the result of a long history of engagement, hostile and otherwise, with white and other Americans. His argument for Afrocentricity supports a larger effort to lift the self-esteem of black people, especially black children. He deploys what Robert Gooding-Williams labels "Afro-kitsch" to further policy initiatives such as Afrocentric education.[35] In framing these arguments, Asante speaks poignantly of a human quest to be "normal and uncomplicated."[36] The existential yearning to be normal is understandable, given the psychological toll that racism can exact. But strategic racial retreat, whether in the form of racial solidarity or personal repose, should never become a place of hibernation.

In this final chapter I have tried to weave together the book's two major theoretical threads: racial randomization and racial navigation. How can the principle of nondiscrimination in adoptive placement be compatible with a race-conscious view of personal identity? To see how these two ideas can coexist and further racial justice in adoption requires that we expand our moral inquiry to cover the wide-angle view of adoption. Social workers should take race into account when making placement decisions, not in the form of barring whites from adopting black children or blacks from adopting white children, but as a way of avoiding naive colorblindness.

Race will be a factor in a black or biracial child's life because she lives in a social environment built on racial categories. But racial imposition is not the end of the story. Black children adopted by whites should be encouraged to recognize their racial classification as a way of making sense of how others perceive them. At the same time, these children should also be given the tools to resist absorbing racial stereotypes. Racial navigation is a metaphor for this taxing but crucial coping mechanism. The publicity of adoption—the involvement of the state—gives us an opportunity to examine the ethics of using race as a proxy for family compatibility. Adoption makes explicit the link between public and private forms of racism. Racial justice in adoption requires that we scrutinize both sides of this social and legal divide. The law, as I have stressed throughout this book, is limited in its ability to change how we think about race in our personal relationships. My hope is that people will appreciate the practical reality of race without turning race into a barrier to family configuration in adoption and beyond.

Conclusion

While I was finishing this book, a television commercial for a Midwestern telephone company caught my eye. The company was advertising a new discount rate for family members who presumably call one another frequently. To emphasize the plan's attractiveness, the commercial featured a succession of groups of people pretending to be families so that they could take advantage of the bargain. One cluster included a short elderly Asian woman flanked by two tall, blond, and white "surfer dudes" who were posing as her sons. Another configuration consisted of an elderly white man standing between twenty-something black male twins. The final scenario was a posse of clean-cut white men standing next to an Asian "brother" with his hair dyed scarlet red.

The telephone company was banking on my snap judgment that each one of these "families" is a fake. What a joke it is to see an old white guy pretending to be the father of young black men. How jarring is the image of an Asian woman mothering white California sunshine boys. An eclectic Asian man in a sea of J. Crew white boys? How strange! The comic basis of this commercial speaks volumes about our familial expectations. We expect family members to physically resemble one another. At a minimum, we expect them to be in the same racial category. The social landscape of the United States has never been free of racial categories, but must that reality prevent us from seeing people of different racial classifications as constituting a legitimate family?

This book has tried to challenge race-based intuitions about which persons belong together in a family. Private racism in the construction of families produces public images that mold social custom. Rarely do we question the morality of these race-based decisions. We perceive this freedom to be a constitutionally protected right to freedom of association. But moral inquiry should not stop at constitutional interpretation. I have argued for a broad-based moral principle of nondiscrimination that applies to all aspects of family life. Adoption provides a useful window onto private racial discrimination in family construction because prospective adopters are prompted by agencies and lawyers to choose children according to racial ascription, along with a host of other characteristics. While race-based preferences in coital reproduction are rarely articulated, they are made indirectly through the selection of a heterosexual partner.

These race-based private decisions are legal but not necessarily morally justified. No causal relationship exists between a person's racial ascription and his or her moral stature, cultural practices, or personality. This is not to say that we should adopt a colorblind approach to adoption, biological reproduction, or social conduct in general. Colorblindness is practically impossible in a race-conscious world, and therefore it is an unrealistic short-term goal. Because we cannot prevent ourselves from noticing the color of someone's skin, colorblindness is a disingenuous refrain that is selectively applied in equal-protection law to ensure prospective adopters the equal opportunity to adopt a black child if they so desire. But these arguments ignore the racial prejudice of prospective adopters, which is declared a private rather than public form of racial discrimination. Supporters of TRA have mostly turned a blind eye to the legal and moral right of children in need of adoption not to be subject to this form of racial classification, which results in black children waiting longer for adoption. The morality of these "private" choices fails to register on the barometer of colorblind constitutionalism.

The thought experiment of racial randomization in adoptive placement is intended to expose our resistance to colorblindness in our personal behavior. A true application of colorblindness in adoption would prevent prospective adopters from choosing children according to their racial classification. Richard Banks argues that states are legally obligated to implement such a policy because when a state classifies children in its custody by race, it engages in a constitutionally prohibited form of state-sponsored racial discrimination that cannot be justified by a compelling state interest. While Banks is right to theoretically press colorblind constitutionalism to its logical end, there are practical reasons for not turning racial randomization into actual public policy.

Such a policy would drive many would-be adopters out of the adoption system altogether, thus depriving children of the permanent homes they may otherwise have had. This is especially important to consider in light of the fact that prospective adopters are increasingly turning to independent, lawyer-mediated domestic and international adoptions that fall outside the jurisdiction of the current federal law banning federally funded agencies from denying or delaying a placement based on race. Prospective adopters who can afford expensive legal fees and value the ability to specify the racial classification of their adoptive child would exit the public adoption system in even greater numbers under racial randomization. The likelihood of massive resistance to racial randomization should make us rethink the social purpose of adoption, as well as our own racially aversive behavior.

While proponents of TRA narrowly focus on issues of "reverse discrimination" in adoption, opponents of TRA make the mistake of using black children in need of adoption to further adult conceptions of black cultural community. These theories of racial solidity are premised on the belief that black individuals should acquire a solid sense of their racial identity from parents who share their racial designation. Advocates of racial solidity often collapse racial ascription into cultural identity and insist that there is a correct bundle of cultural practices that are the "natural" possession of black persons. On this view the adoption of black children by white parents severs intergenerational racial cultural continuity. Theories of racial solidity promote simplistic, one-dimensional approaches to both race and racial self-identification.

Objections to TRA based on a preset notion of black cultural conduct deny the complexity and variation of individual responses to the weight of racial imposition. Race matters, but we need to be careful in thinking about *how* it ought to matter. Racial expectations weigh heavily on our minds and bodies, but we should not think of these expectations as overpowering our capacity to respond to racial ascription in active ways that foster multifaceted self-concepts. Racial self-identification should be a perpetual process of navigation rather than something we "get" from parents, adoptive or original. Unlike constitutional colorblindness, racial navigation is a moral principle that is to guide the entire scope of adoption, especially after placement.

A primary goal of this book is to eschew simplistic, polemical treatments of TRA. Transracial adoptees are individuals whose responses to the involuntary association of interracial adoptive family life will vary from person to person and are likely to change over time. This seemingly obvious point is conspicuously absent from the public debate over TRA. Lawyers, social workers, and scholars have limited their investigation to the event of adoptive placement. While placement is important, analyses of adoption must be able to imagine children in need of adoption as potential adults whose life courses TRA will undoubtedly complicate but not necessarily overwhelm or diminish.

Racial ascription is an involuntary association that affects our self-understandings. But taking race into account need not eviscerate personal agency. The social and legal practice of adoption is a lens through which to examine the idea of situated identity. The political theory method of thought experiment helps us to step back from immediate circumstances, to examine the morality of today's adoption system in a comprehensive way. I have sought to achieve this critical distance without abstracting too much from people's real-life racial experiences at the dawn of twenty-first-century America. My hope is that the compatible principles of racial randomization (nondiscrimination) and racial navigation will supply theoretical insight to those engaged in adoption policymaking and practice.

To be a navigator is to be a problem-solver. We share the enduring problem of racial classification, a social system that too often locks individuals into stereotypes of inferiority. All stereotypes curb human freedom because they reduce individual lives to one-dimensional objects. Racial justice in adoption and in other areas of U.S. life requires that we acknowledge racial existential starting points without permanently retreating into racial boxes. I hope that my argument is not read as a celebration of racial categories. Instead, I have argued for racial recognition as a pragmatic way of addressing racism and its spiraling effects. Racial classification should not be treated as a barrier in either agency placement decisions or adopter choice. We should acknowledge that race is a factor in the lives of all children, while encouraging them to think critically about how racial categories influence their personal understandings and life projects. Rejecting the simplistic assumption that children receive ready-made racial identities from their parents, original or adoptive, is one step in that direction.

Notes

INTRODUCTION

1. Ruth-Arlene Howe, "Transracial Adoption (TRA): Old Prejudices and Discrimination Float under a New Halo," *Boston University Public Interest Law Journal* 6, no.2 (1997),:440 (citing Joyce Ladner, *Mixed Families: Adopting across Racial Boundaries* [1967]).
2. Elizabeth Bartholet, "Where Do Black Children Belong? The Politics of Race Matching in Adoption," *University of Pennsylvania Law Review* 139, no.5 (May 1991): 1180.
3. National Association of Black Social Workers, Position Paper (April 1972), cited in Rita J. Simon, Howard Alstein, and Marygold S. Meiili, *The Case for Transracial Adoption* (Washington: American University Press, 1994), 40.
4. Bartholet, "Where Do Black Children Belong?," 1180. The number of TRAs in this period are not broken down into racial classification. Simon, Altstein, and Melli's estimates are slightly higher than Bartholet's, but there is general agreement among adoption researchers that the numbers of TRAs, especially whites adopting black children, increased during the late 1960s and began to decline in the mid-1970s. Simon et. al., 1.
5. According Simon, Altstein, Melli, the following organizations have compiled national adoption statistics based on surveys of adoption agencies: the Child Welfare League of America (CWLA), the National Center for Health Statistics (NCHS), the National Committee for Adoption (NCFA), and the North American Council for Adoptable Children (NACAC). Simon et. al., 3.
6. Jill Smolowe, "Adoption in Black and White: An Odd Coalition Takes Aim at the Decades-Old Prejudice against Transracial Placements," *Time,* 14 August 1995, 50.
7. Karen Spar, "Foster Care and Adoption Statistics Summary," http://www.casanet.org/library/foster care/fost.htm. These figures do not reflect the actual number of children available for adoption, however,

as not all children in foster care have been legally released from their original families.

8. U.S. Census Bureau, Census 2000 Redistricting Data (P.L. 94–171).

9. James Bowen, "Cultural Convergences and Divergences: The Nexus between Putative Afro-American Family Values and the Best Interests of the Child," *Journal of Family Law* 26, no.3 (1987–88): 493.

10. The most recent data available from the National Council for Adoption indicate that in 1986 31 percent of domestic unrelated adoptions were independent (lawyer mediated). National Council for Adoption (formerly National Committee for Adoption), *Adoption Factbook* (Washington, D.C., June 1989). Cited in Spar, "Foster Care and Adoption Statistics Summary."

11. According to the Immigration and Naturalization Service, there were an estimated 11,340 adoptions of foreign-born children by Americans in 1996. There were 9,670 such adoptions in 1995, 7,093 in 1990, and 9,945 in 1986. Spar, "Foster Care and Adoption Statistics Summary."

12. A 1990 NACAC report based on a 1987 survey stated that TRAs accounted for only 8 percent of all adoptions and that most TRAs involved white adopters and nonblack children. Adoptions involving a white mother and a black child accounted for a mere 1 percent of all adoptions. Simon, *The Case for Transracial Adoption*, 3.

13. Naomi Zack, *Race and Mixed Race* (Philadelphia: Temple University Press, 1993), 40.

14. John Rawls, *A Theory of Justice* (Cambridge, Mass.: Harvard University Press, 1971), 12.

15. Ibid., 13.

16. John Howard Griffin, *Black like Me* (Boston: Houghton Mifflin, 1961).

17. Michael Marriott, "Frank Racial Dialogue Thrives on the Web," *New York Times*, 8 March 1998, 1.

18. W. E. B. Du Bois, *The Souls of Black Folk* (New York: Penguin Books, 1989), 1.

19. Carol Pateman, *The Sexual Contract* (Stanford, Calif.: Stanford University Press, 1988).

20. Charles W. Mills, *The Racial Contract* (Ithaca, N.Y.: Cornell University Press, 1997), 7.

21. "Blacks, for example, constitute only about 1 percent of philosophers in North American universities—a hundred or so people out of more than ten thousand—and there are even fewer Latino, Asian American, and Native American philosophers." Mills, *The Racial Contract*, 2, citing the 1994 report "Status and Future of the Profession," *Proceedings and Addresses of the American Philosophical Association* 70, no.2 (1996): 137.

22. Mills, *The Racial Contract*, 2.

23. Historian David Roediger argues that workers in nineteenth-century

America constructed their sense of whiteness against the situation of slaves by the language they chose to describe themselves: "White female household workers in particular 'resisted' the designation *servant*, in favor of 'helps, helpers or hand'." He explains that "in popularizing such new words, farm and household workers were not simply becoming racists, but neither were they simply being militant republicans. Rather, they were becoming *white workers* who identified their freedom and their dignity in work as being suited to those who were 'not slaves' or 'not ne-gurs.'" *The Wages of Whiteness* (New York: Verso, 1991), 49.

24. Steven A. Holmes, "How Race Is Lived in America," a public forum at the University of Wisconsin-Madison, 14 November 2000.
25. See generally Michel Foucault, *The History of Sexuality*, vol. 1 (New York: Vintage Books, 1990), and *Madness and Civilization: A History of Insanity in the Age of Reason* (New York: Random House, 1965).
26. Section 1808 of the Small Business Job Protection Act of 1996, Pub. Law No. 104–88: Removal of Barriers to Interethnic Adoption.
27. The Howard Metzenbaum Multiethnic Placement Act of 1994, Pub. Law No. 103–06.
28. In 1999, households with incomes below the poverty line included 29.9% of blacks, 27% of Hispanics, 16.7% of whites, and 14% of Asian or Pacific Islanders. www.census.gov/hhes/poverty99/table5.html.
29. Racial disparity in court termination of parental rights has been especially blatant in the criminal prosecution of women who test positive for illegal drug use during pregnancy. For example, in 1989, the Medical University of South Carolina (MUSC), a teaching hospital in Charleston, collaborated with local law-enforcement officials to institute a policy of non-consensual drug testing of pregnant patients, mandatory reporting of positive results to police, and criminal arrest for child abuse and drug possession based on positive test results. Criminal convictions for such felonies were used as the basis for court termination of parental rights. The MUSC serves an indigent and mostly black population in Charleston. It was the only hospital in the city to institute such a policy. See Dorothy Roberts, *Killing the Black Body: Race, Reproduction and, the Meaning of Liberty* (New York: Pantheon Books, 1997), 159–62. On March 21, 2001, the Supreme Court ruled that the practice of non-consensual drug tests for pregnant women violates the Fourth Amendment protection against unreasonable searches. *Crystal M. Ferguson v. City of Charleston* 99 S.Ct. 936 (2001).
30. Mark Courtney, "The Politics and Realities of Transracial Adoption," *Child Welfare* 126, no. 6 (November–December 1997): 757.
31. S. A. Kossoudji, "Pride and Prejudice: Culture's Role in Markets," in *The Question of Discrimination: Racial Inequality in the U.S. Labor Market*, ed. S.

Schulman and W. Darity (Middletown, Conn.: Wesleyan University Press, 1989), 293–314; cited in Courtney, "The Politics and Realities of Transracial Adoption," 756.

32. Courtney, "The Politics and Realities of Transracial Adoption," 757.

CHAPTER 1

1. Michael Omi and Howard Winant, *Racial Formation in the United States: 1960s to the 1990s* (New York: Routledge, 1994).

2. For personal accounts of transracial adoption from the perspective of adult adoptees see Rita J. Simon and Rhonda M. Roorda, *In Their Own Voices: Transracial Adoptees Tell Their Stories* (New York: Columbia University Press, 2000). For personal accounts of being biracial see Lise Funderburg, *Black, White, Other: Biracial Americans Talk About Race and Identity* (New York: William Morrow, 1994). For a thoughtful personal account of having two black biological parents and "looking white" see Toi Derricotte, *The Black Notebooks: An Interior Journey* (New York: W. W. Norton, 1997).

3. Lawrence Wright, "One Drop of Blood," *New Yorker,* July 25, 1994, 47. The U.S. practice of measuring racial demographics is somewhat unique. Canada, by comparison, stopped including racial categories on its census in 1951. Historically, there have been efforts to remove the race question from the U.S. Census. In 1960, the American Civil Liberties Union unsuccessfully pushed for the elimination of racial categories on the census. In 1962 and 1963, New Jersey stopped including racial designations on birth and death certificates. Ibid., 50.

4. Ibid, 52.

5. F. James Davis gives an overview of the staggered emergence of the "one-drop" rule in the antebellum South. While the upper South adopted this rule by the early eighteenth century, southern Louisiana and South Carolina continued to accord mulattos a distinct legal and social status in between that of whites and blacks until the 1850s. Davis argues that by the 1920s, the "one-drop" rule had become uniformly accepted throughout the United States. *Who Is Black? One Nation's Definition* (University Park: Pennsylvania State University Press, 1991), 31–49.

6. In *Behind the Mule: Race and Class in African-American Politics* (Princeton: Princeton University Press, 1994) Michael Dawson argues that black Americans continue to be mostly united in their political attitudes in spite of socioeconomic class divisions among blacks. See also Katherine Tate, *From Protest to Politics: The New Black American Voters in American Elections* (New York: Russell Sage, 1993).

7. Russell Thornton, "What the Census Doesn't Count." *New York Times,* 23 March 2001, A19.

8. Naomi Zack, *Race and Mixed Race* (Philadelphia: Temple University Press, 1993), 14.

9. Ibid., 27.

10. Randall Kennedy draws a distinction between the use of racial proxies by police and private parties. He argues that police should not use race as a proxy for surveillance and interrogation but says that "we should sympathize with, and thus qualify our criticisms of, those [private parties] who do resort to racially discriminatory cues as a stratagem for self-defense." Unlike private parties, police officers are "linked to a bureaucracy able to call upon significant resources for the protection of their agents." The vulnerability of private parties justifies, in Kennedy's view, the use of racial proxies for self-protection. *Race, Crime, and the Law* (New York: Vintage Books, 1997), 165–66.

11. Joseph H. Carens, "Realistic and Idealistic Approaches to the Ethics of Migration," *International Migration Review* 30, no. 1 (Spring 1996): 158.

12. Stephen Jay Gould, *The Mismeasure of Man* (New York: Norton, 1981), 331.

13. Charles Taylor's discussion of dialogical identity construction with "significant others" draws from the work of M. M. Bakhtin. See "The Politics of Recognition," in *Multiculturalism*, ed. Amy Gutmann (Princeton, N.J.: Princeton University Press, 1994).

14. Orlando Patterson, *The Ordeal of Integration* (Washington, D.C.: Civitas, 1997), xi.

15. Richard J. Herrnstein and Charles Murray, *The Bell Curve: Intelligence and Class Structure in American Life* (New York: Free Press, 1994).

16. Scientific theories and classifications varied widely during the early part of the nineteenth century, yet the notion of permanent human types became the most popular. This school of thought supported the prevailing notion that blacks and whites differed from one another in more ways than any other "types," and that this typological difference limited the kinds of social interaction a white person could have with a black person. The following statement made by Abraham Lincoln on August 14, 1862, expresses this brand of scientific racism: "You and we are different races. We have between us a broader difference than exists between any other two races. Whether it is right or wrong I need not discuss, but this physical difference is a great disadvantage to us both, as I think your race suffer very greatly, many of them by living among us, while ours suffer from your presence." Cited in Michael Banton, *The Race Idea* (Cambridge: Tavistock, 1977), 1.

17. Ibid., 5–6.

18. See Stephen W. Mosher, "The Repackaging of Margaret Sanger." Wall Street Journal, 5 May 1997, A18; Adolph Reed, Jr., "The Underclass as Myth and Symbol: The Poverty of Discourse about Poverty," *Radical America* 24 (Winter 1992): 21–40.

19. Michael Omi and Howard Winant, *Racial Formation in the United States* (New York: Routledge, 1989),15.

20. Robert A. Dahl, *Pluralist Democracy in the United States* (Chicago: Rand McNally, 1967); David B. Truman, *The Governmental Process* (New York: Knopf, 1955).

21. E. E. Schattschneider, *The Semisovereign People: A Realist's View of Democracy in America* (New York: Holt, Rinehart, and Winston, 1960). For an account of how black interest group politics has failed to adequately represent "cross-cutting issues" of class, gender, and sexuality, see Cathy J. Cohen, *The Boundaries of Blackness: AIDS and the Breakdown of Black Politics* (Chicago: University of Chicago Press, 1999). See also Dara Z. Strolovitch, "Closer to a Pluralist Heaven? Advocacy Groups, and the Politics of Representation," Ph.D. diss. (New Haven, Conn.: Yale University, Department of Political Science, 2002).

22. Patterson, *The Ordeal of Integration*, 147.

23. Thomas Sowell, *Civil Rights: Rhetoric or Reality?* (New York: William Morrow, 1984).

24. Ibid., 77–79.

25. Omi and Winant, *Racial Formation*, 22.

26. Mary Waters, *Ethnic Options: Choosing Identities in America* (Berkeley: University of California Press, 1990).

27. Patterson, *The Ordeal of Integration*, xi.

28. Ibid., 182.

29. George Kateb, "Response to Robert Gooding-Williams," *Constellations* 5 (March 1998): 48–50, 48.

30. Patricia J. Williams, *Seeing a Color-blind Future: The Paradox of Race (1997 BBC Reith Lectures)* (New York: Noonday Press, 1997), 73.

31. Todd S. Purdum, "California Census Confirms Whites Are in Minority," *New York Times* 30 March 2001, A1.

32. K. Anthony Appiah and Amy Gutmann, *Color Conscious: The Political Morality of Race* (Princeton, N.J.: Princeton University Press, 1996), 33.

33. Ibid.

34. Ibid.

35. Ibid., 49.

36. Gould, *The Mismeasure of Man*, 28–29.

37. Ibid., 330.

38. Ibid., 331.

39. Z. Z. Packer, "Drinking Coffee Elsewhere," *New Yorker*, 19–26 June 2000, 156–70, 156.

40. Appiah and Gutmann, *Color Conscious*, 104. Appiah borrows these nouns from Richard Rorty's *Contingency, Irony, and Solidarity* (New York: Cambridge University Press, 1989).

41. Judith Butler, *Bodies That Matter: On the Discursive Limits of "Sex"* (New York: Routledge, 1993), 125.

42. bell hooks, "Is Paris Burning?," in *Black Looks: Race and Representation* (Boston: South End Press, 1992).

43. Judy Scales-Trent, *Notes of a White Black Woman* (University Park: Pennsylvania State University Press, 1995), 11.

44. Ibid., 19–20.

45. Robert Gooding-Williams, "Race, Multiculturalism, and Democracy," *Constellations* 5, no.1 (1998): 18–41, 21.

46. Appiah, "Identity, Authenticity, Survival: Multicultural Societies and Social Reproduction" in Multiculturalism, ed. Gutaman, 161.

47. Appiah and Gutmann, *Color Conscious*, 98–99.

48. James McBride, *The Color of Water: A Black Man's Tribute to His White Mother* (New York: Riverhead Books, 1996), 103.

49. Jean-Paul Sartre, *Being and Nothingness: An Essay on Phenomenological Ontology* (New York: Philosophical Library, 1956), 363.

50. Shelby Steele, *The Content of our Character: A New Vision of Race in America* (New York: HarperCollins Publishers, 1990), 10.

51. Ibid., 16.

52. Ibid., 15.

53. Glenn C. Loury, *One by One from the Inside Out: Essays and Interviews on Race and Responsibility in America* (New York: Free Press, 1995), 21. See also Shelby Steele, *A Dream Deferred: The Second Betrayal of Black Freedom in America* (New York: HarperPerennial Library, 1999).

54. Gould, *The Mismeasure of Man*, 28, 29.

CHAPTER 2

1. Drucilla Cornell, *Just Cause: Freedom, Identity, and Rights* (New York: Rowman & Littlefield, 2000), 49.

2. I have in mind Larry Blum's definition of *compassion* as a moral sentiment that involves imaginative dwelling on another person's situation. Compassion for Blum is neither pity nor sympathy, both of which tend to instill a feeling of superiority in the observer. When I am compassionate I don't try to put myself in the other person's shoes. Instead, I imagine what it might be like to be that person in her shoes. "Compassion," in *Explaining Emotions*, ed. Amelie O. Rorty (Berkeley: University of California Press, 1980), 507–18.

3. Stanley N. Katz, "The Strange Birth and Unlikely History of Constitutional Equality," *Journal of American History* 75, no. 3 (December 1988): 747–62, 747.

4. Morton Horwitz, *The Transformation of American Law, 1870–1960: The Crisis of Legal Orthodoxy* (New York: Oxford University Press, 1992).

5. Building on William James's pragmatism, Benjamin N. Cardozo argues that judges draw from multiple sources when they decide a case, including prevailing social custom, precedent, and their own personal philosophies of life. Benjamin N. Cardozo, *The Nature of the Judicial Process* (New Haven, Conn.: Yale University Press, 1921).

6. *Plessy v. Ferguson*, 163 U.S. 559 (1896) (Harlan, J., dissenting).

7. 109 U.S. 3 (1883) (Harlan, J., dissenting).

8. 109 U.S. 3 (1883).

9. 407 U.S. 163 (1972).

10. 111 S.Ct. 2077 (1986).

11. 457 U.S. 922 (1982).

12. 111 S.Ct. 2077 (1991).

13. Whether and to what degree courts can influence social change, both as a historical and future matter, has been hotly debated among political scientists and legal theorists. Gerald Rosenberg argues that *Brown v. Board* of Education was not the most powerful factor in bringing and an end to legally mandated racial segregation in public schools. Gerald N. Rosenberg, *The Hollow Hope: Can Courts Bring About Social Change?* (Chicago: University of Chicago Press), 1991. Other scholars have emphasized the symbolic power of *Brown*. See for example, Stephen L. Carter, "Do Courts Matter?" 90 *Michigan Law Review* (1992), 1216.

14. Twila Perry, "The Transracial Adoption Controversy: An Analysis of Discourse and Subordination," *New York University Review of Law and Social Change* 21, no.1 (1993–94): 33–108, 49.

15. Bartholet, "Where Do Black Children Belong? The Politics of Race Matching in Adoption," *University of Pennsylvania Law Review* 139 (1991): 1163–1256, 1251, 245n.

16. See, for example, John Rawls, *A Theory of Justice* (Cambridge, Mass.: Harvard University Press, 1971); Amy Gutmann and Dennis Thompson, *Democracy and Disagreement* (Cambridge, Mass.: Harvard University Press, 1996), chap. 8.

17. Elisabeth Landes and Richard Posner, "The Economics of the Baby Shortage," *Journal of Legal Studies* 7 (1978): 323–48.

18. Ibid., 344, citing *Economics and the Family*, ed. Theodore W. Schultz (Cambridge, Mass.: National Bureau of Economic Research, 1974).

19. Rebecca Carroll, afterword to Jan Waldron, *Giving Away Simone* (New York: Random House, 1995), 233–34.

20. Richard Posner, *Sex and Reason* (Cambridge, Mass.: Harvard University Press, 1992), 415.

21. Ibid., 410.

22. Ibid., 413.

23. Rita J. Simon, Howard Alstein, and Marygold S. Melli, *The Case For Transracial Adoption* (Washington: American University Press, 1994), 11.

24. http://www.instituteforjustice.org.

25. Ibid.

26. Clint Bolick, "Clinton's Quota Queen," *Wall Street Journal*, 30 April 1993, A12.

27. See, for example, Rebecca Carroll and Bill Dockery, "The Debate over Cross-Racial Adoption: An Odd Coalition Takes Aim at the Decades-Old Prejudice against Transracial Placements," *USA Magazine*, 7–19 March 1995; Lena Williams, " "Losing Isaiah": Truth in Shades of Grey," *New York Times*, 23 March 1995, C1; Jill Smolowe, "Adoption in Black and White," *Time*, 14 August 1995.

28. Howard M. Metzenbaum Multiethnic Placement Act of 1994, 42 U.S.C.

29. Stephen Holmes, "Bitter Racial Dispute Rages Over Adoption," A16.

30. Institute for Justice, "Opposition Motion" (filed in Travis County, Texas, district court), *Boston University Public Interest Law Journal* 6, no.2 (Winter 1997): 473–525, 481.

31. This administrative interpretation was consistent with Section 553 of the federal law, the Howard Metzenbaum Multiethnic Placement of 1994, P.L. 103–06. Section 553 of this law was repealed by Section 1808 of the Small Business Job Protection Act of 1996.

32. Institute for Justice, "Opposition Motion."

33. Institute for Justice, "Opposition Motion," 489. Citing *Miller v. Johnson*, 115 S.Ct. 2475, 2482 (1995) and *Regents of University of California v. Bakke*, 438 U.S. 265, 291 (1978).

34. Randall Kennedy, "Orphans of Separatism: The Painful Politics of Transracial Adoption," *American Prospect* no.17 (Spring 1994): 38–45, 41.

35. Bartholet, "Where Do Black Children Belong?," 1227.

36. Institute for Justice, "Opposition Motion," 489.

37. Ibid., 48914n.

38. Elizabeth Bartholet, *Nobody's Children: Abuse and Neglect, Foster Drift, and the Adoption Alternative* (Boston: Beacon Press, 1999), 134–37.

39. Ibid.

40. Ibid., 134.

41. Ibid., 131.

42. In *Village of Arlington Heights v. Metropolitan Housing Development Corp.*, 429 U.S. at 152 (1977), the black plaintiffs "simply failed to carry their burden of proving that discriminatory purpose was a motivating factor in the Village's decision." Charles Lawrence argues that "the law should be equally concerned when the mind's censor successfully disguises a socially repugnant wish like racism if that motive produces behavior that

has a discriminatory result as injurious as if it flowed from a consciously held motive." "The ID, the EGO, and Equal Protection: Reckoning with Unconscious Racism."

43. *Rogers v. American Airlines* 252 F. Supp. 229 (S.D.N.Y 1981) upheld the right of an employer to ban braided hairstyles as a condition of employment. A black woman who wore her hair in braids filed suit alleging that American Airlines had discriminated against her as a black woman. The court based its decision on the distinction between cultural and biological notions of race instead of looking at the discriminatory impact of the policy. See Paulette M. Caldwell, "A Hair Piece: Perspectives on the Intersection of Race and Gender," in *Critical Race Feminism*, ed. Adrienne Wing (New York: Routledge, 1997).

44. Kimberle Crenshaw, "Race, Reform, and Retrenchment: Transformation and Legitimization in Anti-Discrimination Law," *Harvard Law Review* 101, no. 1331 (1988).

45. U.S. Department of Health and Human Services Administration of Children, Youth, and Families, Information Memorandum to State and Territorial Agencies Administrating Title IV-B and Title IV-E of the Social Security Act. Information on Implementation of Federal Legislation.

46. Joan Hollinger, "A Guide to the Multiethnic Placement Act of 1994, As Amended by the Interethnic Adoption Provisions of 1996." http//:www.acf.dhhs.gov.programs/cb/special.mepachp3.htm

47. See for example Sally Haslanger, "You Mixed? Racial Identity Without Racial Biology," in eds. Sally Haslanger and Charlotte Witt, *The View From Home: Philosophical and Feminist Issues in Adoption* (Boulder, Col.: Westview Press, 2002); Sharon Rush, *Loving Across the Color Line: A White Adoptive Mother Learns About Race* (Lanham. MD: Rowman and Littlefield, 2000).

CHAPTER 3

1. William T. Merritt, speech to the 1971 National Association of Black Social Workers National Conference, Washington, D.C. Cited in Rita J. Simon, Howard Altstein, and Marygold S. Melli, *The Case for Transracial Adoption* (Washington: American University Press, 1994), 40.

2. William T. Merritt, excerpt from testimony by William T. Merritt, president of the National Association of Black Social Workers, during U.S. Senate Hearings of the Committee on Labor and Human Resources, 25 June 1985 Cited in Ibid.

3. National Association of Black Social Workers, *Position Statement: Preserving African American Families* (Detroit: National Association of Black Social Workers, 1994).

4. Twila Perry recommends that "newborns be placed in foster care for a period of no more than six months while the agency seeks an adoptive family of the same race. Upon expiration of that period, if the child has not been placed for adoption, and the foster parents desire to adopt the child, the adoption could not be precluded on the basis of race. Of course, if the foster parents do not wish to adopt and a family of the child's race is later found, the child could be removed from the foster home to be adopted on the basis of the general principle that a permanent home is superior to a temporary one. This principle would govern that situation even if race was not a factor. After the six-month period, if a family of the same race has not been found, the child must be placed in an available adoptive home even if that home is transracial." "Race and Child Placement," *Journal of Family Law* 29 (1993–94): 51–127,124. James Bowen concedes that TRA is preferable to institutional foster care but argues strongly in favor of race-matching placement ("Cultural Convergences and Divergences," 487).

5. Omi and Winant, *Racial Formation in the United States*, 37.

6. Paul Gilroy, *The Black Atlantic: Modernity and Double-Consciousness* (Cambridge, Mass.: Harvard University Press, 1993).

7. For a critical analysis of hip-hop culture see Tricia Rose, *Black Noise: Rap Music and Culture in Contemporary Black America* (Wesleyan, Mass.: Wesleyan University Press, 1994).

8. See the introduction to John Bracey, August Meier, and Elliott Rudwick, *Black Nationalism in America* (New York: Bobbs-Merrill, 1970).

9. Ibid., xxvi.

10. Ibid.

11. Ibid.

12. Ibid.

13. To date, four major surges of black nationalist ideology have sprouted during the following historical periods: 1790–1820, the late 1840s (particularly the 1850s), 1880–1920s, and the mid-1960s-to the early 1970s (ibid., xxv–xxvi).

14. Adam Clayton Powell first used the term *Black Power* in a 1965 Chicago rally. Kwame Ture, then known as Stokely Carmichael, picked up the term and popularized it within the radical wing of the civil rights movement. See Harold Cruse, *The Crisis of the Negro Intellectual* (New York: William Morrow, 1967), 545.

15. I borrow the term "aversive racism" from Joel Kovel, who defines it as reluctance expressed by whites about engaging in intimacy of any kind with blacks. This aversion was contrasted against dominative racism, which describes a violent reaction to the perceived threat of blacks. Joel Kovel, *White Racism: A Psychohistory* (New York: Vintage Books, 1970). For

an overview of different kinds of racism in socio-psychological studies, see Gerard Kleinpenning and Louk Hagendoorn, "Forms of Racism and the Cumulative Dimension of Ethnic Attitudes," *Social Psychology Quarterly* 56 (March 1993): 21–36.

16. Kwame Ture (formerly known as Stokely Carmichael) and Charles V. Hamilton, *Black Power: The Politics of Liberation* (New York: Random House, 1967; rpt., 1992).

17. See Gloria T. Hull, Patricia Bell Scott, and Barbara Smith, *All the Women are White, All the Blacks are Men, But Some of Us are Brave* (Old Westbury, NY.: Feminist Press, 1982); Audre Lorde, *Sister Outsider: Essays and Speeches* (Trumansburg, NY: Crossing Press, 1984); Patricia Hill Collins, *Fighting Back: Black Women and the Search for Justice* (Minneapolis: University of Minnesota Press, 1998); Beverly Guy-Sheftall, ed., *Words of Fire: an Anthology of African American Feminist Thought* (New York: New Press, 1995).

18. Jacob Weisberg, "For the Sake of Argument," *New York Times Magazine*, 5 November 2000, 48, 53.

19. See for example, Edward Banfield, *The Unheavenly City: The Nature and Future of Our Urban Crisis* (Boston: Little and Brown, 1970); Charles Murray, *Losing Ground: American Social Policy, 1950–1980* (New York: Basic Books, 1984); Lawrence Mead, *Beyond Entitlement: The Social Obligations of Citizenship* (New York: Free Press, 1986). All draw on Moynihan's "tangle of pathology" thesis to argue that poverty among blacks living in the "inner city" is largely a function of cultural "tendencies" and behavioral patterns that cannot be ameliorated by public policy; indeed, they maintain that anti-poverty programs of the 1940s and 1960s exacerbated black urban poverty by creating a "culture of dependency." There have been numerous critiques of this argument. For a critique of the use of "dependency" in the above arguments see Nancy Fraser and Linda Gordon, "A Genealogy of *Dependency*: Tracing a Keyword of the U.S. Welfare State," 19 *Signs: Journal of Women in Culture and Society* (Winter 1994): 309–336. For an exploration of how black masculinity is constructed through "culture of poverty" political discourse see Willie M. Legette, "The Crisis of the Black Male: A New Ideology in Black Politics," in Adolph Reed Jr., ed., *Without Justice For All: The New Liberalism and Our Retreat From Racial Equality* (Boulder, Col.: Westview Press, 1999): 291–324.

20. For a critical discussion of black masculinity and the ways in which art can challenge and reinforce stereotypes of black men see the catalog to *Black Male: Representations of Masculinity in Contemporary American Art* (New York: Whitney Museum of Art, 1994).

21. Omi and Winant, *Racial Formation*, 40.

22. David W. Blight and Robert Gooding-Williams, eds., introduction to W.E.B. Du Bois, *The Souls of Black Folk* (New York: Bedford Books, 1997), 13.

23. W.E.B. Du Bois, "The Conservation of Races," in *The Souls of Black Folk*, 230.

24. Ruth-Arlene Howe, "Transracial Adoption (TRA): Old Prejudices and Discrimination Float under a New Halo," *Boston University Public Interest Law Journal* 6, no.2 (Winter 1997): 409–72, 471.

25. Charles Mills, *The Racial Contract* (Ithaca, N.Y.: Cornell University Press, 1997).

26. Bowen, "Cultural Convergences and Divergences," 510.

27. Kevin Gaines, "Race and Racism," *Social Text* 42, no.45 (1995):45–52, 52n33.

28. Rita J. Simon, Howard Altstein, and Marygold S. Melli, *The Case for Transracial Adoption* (Washington, D.C.: American University Press, 1994), 115.

29. K.M. DeBerry, S. Scarr, and R. Weinberg, "Family Racial Socialization and Ecological Competence: Longitudinal Assessments of African American Transracial Adoptees," *Child Development* 67 (1996): 2375–2399.

30. Arlene Skolnick, *Embattled Paradise: The American Family in an Age of Uncertainty* (New York: Basic Books, 1991), xvi.

31. Martha Minow, *Not Only for Myself: Identity, Politics, and the Law* (New York: New Press, 1997), 112.

32. Bartholet, "Where Do Black Children Belong?," 1231.

33. Dorothy E. Roberts, *Killing the Black Body: Race, Reproduction, and the Meaning of Liberty* (New York: Random House, 1997), 262.

34. Minow, *Not Only for Myself*, 29.

35. Many commentators on adoption, and of child welfare in general, have pointed out the malleability of the "best interests of the child" legal standard. Margaret Howard remarks that "despite its vagueness, however, the best interests test does begin to provide some guidance for resolution of these conflicts [between a child's interest in a stable, permanent home and a cultural identity] by emphasizing the individual child's interests, rather than those of adoptive children in general or the institutional interests of minority groups or adoption agencies." "Transracial Adoption: Analysis of the Best Interests Standard," *Notre Dame Law Review* 59 (1984): 503–55, 545. Joseph Goldstein, Albert Solnit, Sonja Goldstein, and Anna Freud argue that we should replace the "best interests" standard with "one that provides the *least detrimental available alternative for safeguarding a child's growth and development*." They argue persuasively that "[a] child whose placement must be determined in legal controversy has already been deprived of her 'best interests'—by the loss or threat of loss of her

parents; by their rejection, neglect, or abuse; or by the breaking up of her family for other reasons. It is beyond any court's power to undo the disturbances that she has already suffered. Acknowledging this fact by the words 'least detrimental' is intended to remind decision-makers that their task is to salvage as much as possible out of a less-than-satisfactory situation." *The Best Interests of the Child: The Least Detrimental Alternative* (New York: Free Press, 1996), 50.

36. Perry, "The Transracial Adoption Controversy," 68.

37. Ibid.

38. Harold Cruse, *The Crisis of the Negro Intellectual* (New York: William Morrow, 1967), 548.

39. I borrow the term "manifesto of identity" from E.U. Essien-Udom, *Black Nationalism: A Search for Identity in America* (Chicago: University of Chicago Press, 1962), 328. In his discussion of black nationalist poetry of the 1960s Black Arts Movement, Phillip Brian Harper puts a new twist on John Stuart Mill's claim that poetry is always overheard. Harper posits that while black nationalist poetry by, for example, Amiri Baraka, may appear to be aimed at a black audience and thus overheard by whites, the opposite may be true. This poetry may be aimed at a white audience and meant to be overheard by Blacks, as distinguished from Negroes, who are already racially conscious. Hence the distinction between Blacks and Negroes; Negroes are lumped together with whites, neither of whom realize that it's "Nation time!" Phillip Brian Harper, *Are We Not Men? Masculine Anxiety and the Problem of African-American Identity* (New York: Oxford University Press, 1996), 45–46.

40. Michael Walzer, *What It Means to Be an American: Essays on the American Experience* (New York: Marsilio, 1996), 3.

41. Walzer does discuss the case of black Americans in *Spheres of Justice* on the question of "the reservation of office." There he argues in favor of reserving offices for blacks as a temporary measure that is to be stopped "as soon as blacks escape from the trap that their blackness has become in a society with a long history of racism." Such a policy is feasible in the United States because it merely reiterates hierarchy rather than challenging or reforming hierarchy. Reserving offices for a group occupying the lowest rung on the ladder will end up hurting the group occupying the next-to-last rung. In the last line of a footnote, Walzer provocatively suggests that monetary reparations to blacks to compensate them for the effects of past racism might be a better form of compensation than the reservation of offices because it would distribute the burden of payment among all citizens. *Spheres of Justice* (New York: Basic Books, 1983), 152–54.

42. Walzer, *What It Means to Be an American*, 4–5.

43. Ibid.

44. Jefferson's famous "wall of separation between church and state" was given emphasis for the first time in the 1947 Supreme Court Case *Everson v. Board of Education of Ewing Township*, 330 U.S. 1 (1946). See Michael Sandel, *Articles of Faith, Articles of Peace* (Washington, D.C.: Brookings Institution, 1990), 81.

45. Walzer, *What It Means to Be an American*, 7.

46. In *City of Richmond v. J. A. Croson Co.*, 488 U.S. 469 (1989), the Supreme Court under Chief Justice William H. Rehnquist found Richmond's local affirmative action plan in city contracting in violation of the Fourteenth Amendment's equal-protection clause. In *Adarand Constructors, Inc. v. Pena*, 115 S.Ct. 2097 (1995), the Supreme Court held that the "strict scrutiny" standard applied in *Croson* also applies to federal affirmative action programs, thus overruling *Metro Broadcasting, Inc. v. Federal Communications Commission* 497 U.S. 547 (1990). For a summary of court rulings and referendums that have challenged and overturned race-based admissions programs in higher education, see Jodi Wilogoren, "U.S. Court Bars Race as Factor In School Entry," *New York Times*, 28 March 2001, A1.

47. In his latest book, *We Are All Multiculturalists Now*, Glazer recants his former anti-affirmative action stance, which was based on his faith that the 1964 Civil Rights Act and the 1965 Voting Rights Act would be sufficient to assimilate blacks into the "mainstream." Christopher Lehmann-Haupt, "A Multiculturalist with Regrets," *New York Times*, 20 March 1997, C18.

48. In a footnote, Walzer writes, "The current demand of (some) black Americans that they be called African Americans represents an attempt to adapt themselves to the ethnic paradigm—imitating, perhaps, the relative success of various Asian-American groups in a similar adaptation" (*What It Means to Be an American*, 44–4530n).

49. Toni Morrison, *Playing in the Dark: Whiteness and the Literary Imagination* (Cambridge, Mass.: Harvard University Press, 1992), 52.

50. See Dalton Conley, *Being Black, Living in the Red* (Berkeley: University of California Press, 1999). Conley demonstrates that wealth disparity between blacks and whites affects socioeconomic stratification far more than measures of income disparity between the two racial groups. A black family and white family may have income parity but whites are far more likely to possess greater wealth (assets). For an exploration of racism from a psychoanalytic perspective, see Joel Kovel, *White Racism: A Psychohistory* (New York: Vintage Books, 1970).

51. Ronald Takaki, *A Different Mirror: A History of Multicultural America* (Boston: Little, Brown, 1993), 5. The relationship between race and ethnic-

ity in the urban uprising that followed the Rodney King verdict are discussed in Robert Gooding-Williams, ed., *Reading Rodney King/Reading Urban Uprising* (New York: Routledge 1993).

52. Takaki, *A Different Mirror*, 8.

53. Charles Taylor, "Multiculturalism and the Politics of Recognition" in *Multiculturalism*, ed. Amy Gutmann (Princeton, N.J.: Princeton University Press, 1992).

54. Ibid., 35.

55. Ibid., 25.

56. Ibid., 65–66.

57. Frantz Fanon, *Black Skin, White Masks* (New York: Grove Press, 1952; rpt., 1967), 116.

58. Fanon, *The Wretched of the Earth* (New York: Grove Press, 1961; rpt., 1963), 122.

59. The term *life script* is taken from K. Anthony Appiah's essay "Identity, Authenticity, Survival: Multicultural Societies and Social Reproduction," in *Multiculturalism*, ed. Gutmann, and is derived from Charles Taylor's theory of dialogical identity formation. See Taylor, "Multiculturalism and the Politics of Recognition."

60. Appiah, "Identity, Authenticity, Survival," 161.

61. Taylor, "Multiculturalism and the Politics of Recognition," 58–59.

62. Will Kymlicka, *Liberalism, Community, and Culture* (New York: Oxford University Press, 1989), 172.

63. Taylor, "Multiculturalism and the Politics of Recognition," 32–33.

64. Lawrence Blum, "Multicultural Education as Values in Education," *Working Papers: Harvard Children's Initiative* (Cambridge, 1997), 7.

65. Amitai Etzioni, ed., *The Essential Communitarian Reader* (New York: Rowman & Littlefield, 1998), xiii.

66. See Michael J. Sandel, *Democracy's Distrust: America in Search of a Public Philosophy* (Cambridge, Mass.: Harvard University Press, 1996); Mary Ann Glendon, *Rights Talk: The Impoverishment of Political Discourse* (New York: Free Press, 1991); Jean Bethke Elshtain, *Democracy on Trial* (New York: BasicBooks, 1995).

67. Waldron, "Minority Cultures and the Cosmopolitan Alternative," 95.

68. Mary Lyndon Shanley, "Unencumbered Individuals and Embedded Selves: Reasons to Resist Dichotomous Thinking in Family Law," in *Debating Democracy's Distrust*, ed. Anita Allen and Milton Regan (New York: Oxford University Press, 1998), 246.

69. Ibid. 242.

70. Rick Thoma estimates that twenty-five to thirty-five percent of Indian children were removed from their homes by state, county, and local social services agencies prior to the 1978 ICWA. Many argue that the ICWA is

not working. Large numbers of Indian children (20–30%) continue to be removed from their original homes and placed with non-Indian parents because social service agencies have not focused their efforts on preserving Indian families. Rick Thoma, "Under Siege: the Indian Child Welfare Act of 1978," *Lifting the Veil: Examining the Child Welfare, Foster Care, and Juvenile Justice Systems*, http://home.rica.net/rthoma/icwa.htm.

71. Shanley, 245.

72. Cynthia Crossen, "Hard Choices: In Today's Adoptions, the Biological Parents Are Calling the Shots," *Wall Street Journal*, 14 September 1989, 1.

CHAPTER 4

1. John Neufeld, *Edgar Allen* (New York: Signet, 1969), 43.

2. Richard Banks, "The Color of Desire: Fulfilling Adoptive Parents' Racial Preferences through Discriminatory State Action," *Yale Law Journal* 107 (1998): 875–964.

3. Rita J. Simon and Rhonda M. Roorda, *In Their Own Voices: Transracial Adoptees Tell Their Stories* (New York: Columbia University Press, 2000).

4. Adoption Exhibit 19A, Race/Ethnicity of Children Awaiting Adoption (Question 21), VCIS Survey 1990 to 1994, Qualified Reporting States Totals and National Estimates, http://www.acf.dhhs.gov/programs/cb/stats/vcis/iv19a.htm.

5. Jill Smolowe, "Adoption in Black and White: An Odd Coalition Takes Aim at the Decades-Old Prejudice against Transracial Placements," *Time*, 14 August 1995, 50.

6. See Carol Stack, *All Our Kin: Strategies For Survival In a Black Community* (New York: Harper and Row, 1974).

7. See Esther B. Fein, "Secrecy and Stigma No Longer Clouding Adoptions," *New York Times*, 25 October, 1998, 1.

8. *Loving v. Virginia*, 388 U.S. 1 (1967).

9. Banks, "The Color of Desire," 881.

10. Ibid.

11. Domestic workers are not parents in any legal sense, and their function is clearly demarcated as facilitating the labor power of their employers, while simultaneously engaged in their own labor production. For a discussion of black women's work as domestic laborers, see Hazel V. Carby, "White Women Listen! Black Feminism and the Boundaries of Sisterhood," in *Black British Cultural Studies*, ed. Houston A. Baker et al. (Chicago: University of Chicago Press, 1996), 61–86.

12. Kim McLarin, "Primary Colors: The Mother Is Black; Her Interracial Daughter Is Fair-Skinned, Society Has Trouble Seeing Their Connection," *New York Times Magazine*, 24 March 1998, 58.

13. Banks qualifies this position by stating that such an exemption might be

too controversial to implement. As a "practical solution," he would ban all race-based adoptive choice (Banks, "The Color of Desire," 944). Nonetheless, his theoretical reasons for exempting blacks from racial randomization deserve attention.

14. See for example Dirk Johnson, "Former Cocaine User Regains Child in Racial Custody Case," *New York Times*, 9 March 1999, A18; Lena Williams, "Beyond *Losing Isaiah*: Truth in Shades of Gray," *New York Times*, 23 March 1995, C1; Jill Smolowe, "Adoption in Black and White," *Time*, 14 August 1995, 50–51; Karin D. Berry, "Adoption, Race, and Red Tape," *Emerge*, April 1995, 40–46.

15. Banks, "The Color of Desire," 944.

16. Margaret Jane Radin, "Market Inalienability," 100 *Harvard Law Review* 1849 (June 1987), 1926. Elizabeth Anderson takes a similar position, arguing against commercial surrogacy on the grounds that it "constitutes an unconscionable commodification of children and of women's reproductive capacities." In Anderson's view, this commodification violates the Kantian imperative to treat other persons as ends rather than as means. Elizabeth S. Anderson, "Is Women's Labor a Commodity?" *Philosophy and Public Affairs* 19 (1990), 71.

17. Mary Lyndon Shanley, *Making Babies, Making Families: What Matters Most In An Age of Reproductive Technologies, Surrogacy, Adoption, and Same-Sex and Unwed Parents* (Boston: Beacon Press, 2001), 41.

18. There has recently been some controversy over which party, the original mother or the adopters, is the client, and whether a conflict of interest arises when lawyers mediate between original mothers and adopters.

19. In Nella Larson's novella *Passing*, light-skinned black women agonize over having children because of the possibility that their recessive genes for darker pigmentation will become dominant in their children: "After taking up her own glass she informed them: 'No, I have no boys and I don't think I'll ever have any. I'm afraid. I nearly died of terror the whole nine months before Margery was born for fear that she might be dark. Thank goodness, she turned out all right. But I'll never risk it again. Never! The strain is simply too—too hellish." In *Quicksand and Passing* (New Brunswick, N.J.: Rutgers University Press, 1986), 168.

20. U.S. Census Bureau, *Statistical Abstract of the United States: 2000*, "No. 54. Married Couples of Same or Mixed Races and Origins: 1980–1999."

21. Victoria Benning and Philip Bennett, "Racial Lines Shadow New Generation," *Boston Globe*, 13 September 1992, 1, 30–31; cited in Maureen T. Reddy, *Crossing the Color Line: Race, Parenting, and Culture* (New Brunswick, N.J.: Rutgers University Press, 1994), 8.

22. Reddy, 10.

23. Bartholet, "Where Do Black Children Belong?," 11738n. This "match-

ing" of light-skinned black children with white adopters also reflects racist prejudice against dark-skinned black children.

24. Microsort is a trademarked technology that has been used in cattle breeding for a decade. It is not yet considered safe for human use, but clinical trials are being performed by the Genetics and I.V.F. Institute. In the first 111 uses of Microsort in humans, eighty-three selected for females and only twenty-eight for males (Lisa Belkin, "Getting the Girl," 29).

25. Reva Siegel, "The Racial Rhetorics of Colorblind Constitutionalism: The Case of *Hopwood v. Texas*," in *Race and Representation: Affirmative Action*, ed. Robert Post and Michael Rogin (New York: Zone Press, 1998), 52.

26. Robin West agrees with Jana Singer that "the denial of the communitarian nature of the family and of marriage has resulted, among much else, in the transformation of family law from a branch of public law into a branch of private law within which parenting is construed as the exercise of consumer choice among an array of social, natural, or technological possibilities." Robin West, "Universalism, Liberal Theory, and the Problem of Gay Marriage," 25 *Florida State University Law Review* (Summer 1998), 723.

27. "What is created through the delegation of privacy to the family, in the name of individual autonomy, is not necessarily individual freedom, but at least for many, its opposite: a Hobbesian state of nature, within which the strong control, by virtue of their superior strength, and the weak, Stockholm-syndrome-like, learn to comply." Ibid. Using law to reinforce the privacy of families also perpetuates an unjust division of labor within households. See Susan Moller Okin, *Justice, Gender, and the Family* (New York: Basic Books, 1989).

28. For a discussion of this central debate in public law, see John Hart Ely, *Democracy and Distrust: A Theory of Judicial Review* (Cambridge, Mass.: Harvard University Press, 1980). Ely argues that judiciary review should be limited to reinforcing the participation of citizens in the democratic process, that courts should not become involved in "the substantive merits of the political choice under attack" (181).

29. 198 U.S. 45, 25 S.Ct. 539 (1905). In his famous dissenting opinion, Justice Oliver Wendell Holmes insisted that the extratextual basis for the majority's decision was "an economic theory which a large part of the country does not entertain"—namely, laissez-faire capitalism.

30. 410 U.S. 113, 93 S.Ct. 705 (1973). Justice Harry A. Blackmun, writing for the Court, notes that "the Constitution does not explicitly mention any right of privacy." Blackmun then points, however, to judicial precedent in which the Court recognized a right to personal privacy in various contexts: "This right of privacy, whether it be founded in the Fourteenth Amendment's concept of personal liberty and restrictions upon state action, as we feel it is, or, as the District Court determined, in the Ninth

Amendment's reservation of rights to the people, is broad enough to encompass a woman's decision whether or not to terminate her pregnancy."

31. 391 U.S. 145, 85 S.Ct. 1678 (1965).
32. Ibid.
33. Patricia Irwin Johnston, *Adopting after Fertility* (Indianapolis: Perspectives Press, 1992), 129–30.
34. Bartholet, *Family Bonds*, 164–65.
35. Neufeld, *Edgar Allen*, 43.

CHAPTER 5

1. Jean-Paul Sartre, *Anti-Semite and Jew* (New York: Schocken Books, 1948).
2. Evelyn Brooks Higginbotham, "African-American Women's History and the Metalanguage of Race," *Signs: Journal of Women in Culture and Society* 17, no.2 (Winter 1992): 267.
3. Michael Walzer, Preface to *Anti-Semite and Jew*, xxiv.
4. Ibid., xxi.
5. Jean-Paul Sartre, *Black Orpheus*, trans. S.W. Allen (Paris: Presence Africaine, 1963).
6. Abiola Irele, "What Is Négritude?," in *The African Experience in Literature and Ideology* (Bloomington: Indiana University Press, 1990), 72.
7. Sartre, *Black Orpheus*, 31.
8. K. Anthony Appiah, *In My Father's House: Africa in the Philosophy of Culture* (New York: Oxford University Press, 1992), 76.
9. Michael Walzer, "On Involuntary Association," in *Freedom of Association*, ed. Amy Gutmann (Princeton, N.J.: Princeton University Press, 1998), 65.
10. *Secret Daughter* aired in November 1996 on *Frontline*, the PBS documentary series.
11. Transcribed in June Cross, "Secret Daughter," *Radcliffe Quarterly*, Winter 1997, 28.
12. I borrow the term *life script* from K. Anthony Appiah, "Identity, Authenticity, Survival" in Amy Gutmann, ed. *Multiculturalism* (Princeton: Princeton University Press, 1994), 161.
13. Orlando Patterson, *Slavery and Social Death* (Cambridge, Mass.: Harvard University Press, 1982), 5.
14. Howe, "Transracial Adoption (TRA)," 423.
15. Sartre, *Black Orpheus*, 15.
16. Catherine McKinley and Kai Jackson, "Sisters: A Reunion Story," in *The Adoption Reader*, ed. Susan Wadia-Ells (Seattle: Seal Press, 1995), 196.
17. Jeremy Waldron, "What Is Cosmopolitan?" *Journal of Political Philosophy* 8 (2000), 232.
18. Ibid., 235.
19. See Jeremy Waldron, "Minority Cultures and the Cosmopolitan Alterna-

tive," in *The Rights of Minority Cultures*, ed. Will Kymlicka (New York: Oxford University Press, 1995): 93–119.

20. Waldron, "What Is Cosmopolitan?," 228.

21. Ibid.

22. Ibid., 231.

23. Based on 2000 Census data, blacks, Latinos, Asians, and whites continue to live apart from one another in New York City, while the city's suburbs have become more racially diverse. Janny Scott, "Races Still Tend to Live Apart in New York, Census Shows," *New York Times* 23 March 2001, B1.

24. Iris Marion Young, *Justice and the Politics of Difference* (Princeton, N.J.: Princeton University Press, 1990).

25. Ibid., 239.

26. Ibid., 256.

27. K. Anthony Appiah, "Cosmopolitan Patriots," in *For Love of Country: Debating the Limits of Patriotism*, ed. Martha Nussbaum (Boston: Beacon Press, 1996), 22–23.

28. Appiah, citing Richard Rorty's *Contingency, Irony, and Solidarity* (New York: Cambridge University Press, 1989), in Appiah and Gutmann, *Color Conscious*, 104.

29. Appiah and Gutmann, *Color Conscious*, 90.

30. Molefi Kete Asante, "Racism, Consciousness, and Afrocentricity," in *Lure and Loathing: Essays on Race, Identity, and the Ambivalence of Assimilation*, ed. Gerald Early (New York: Penguin Press, 1993), 137

31. Ibid., 141.

32. Ibid, 139.

33. Sartre, *Black Orpheus*, 15.

34. Ibid.

35. "Asante speaks the language of kitsch because he invokes the imagery of a fixed biological identity to construct a putatively equal image of African-American cultural identity." Robert Gooding-Williams, "Race, Multiculturalism, and Democracy," *Constellations* 5, no.1 (March 1998): 28.

36. Asante, "Racism, Consciousness, and Afrocentricity," 143.

Bibliography

Abiola, Irele. *The African Experience in Literature and Ideology*. Bloomington: Indiana University Press, 1990.

Allen, Anita, and Milton Regan, eds. *Debating Democracy's Distrust*. New York: Oxford University Press, 1998.

Anderson, Elizabeth S. "Is Women's Labor A Commodity?" *Philosophy and Public Affairs* 19 (1990): 71–92.

Appiah, K. Anthony. *In My Father's House: Africa in the Philosophy of Culture*. New York: Oxford University Press, 1992.

Appiah, K. Anthony, and Amy Gutmann. *Color Conscious: The Political Morality of Race*. Princeton, N.J.: Princeton University Press, 1996.

Baker, Houston, Jr.; Manthia Diawara; and Ruth Lindeborg, eds. *Black British Cultural Studies: A Reader*. Chicago: University of Chicago Press, 1996.

Banfield, Edward. *The Unheavenly City: The Nature and Future of Our Urban Crisis*. Boston: Little and Brown, 1970.

Banks, Richard. "The Color of Desire: Fulfilling Adoptive Parents' Racial Preferences through Discriminatory State Action." *Yale Law Journal* 107 (1998): 875–964.

Banton, Michael. *The Idea of Race*. Cambridge: Tavistock, 1977.

Bartholet, Elizabeth. *Nobody's Children: Abuse and Neglect, Foster Drift, and the Adoption Alternative*. Boston: Beacon Press, 1999.

——. "Beyond Biology: The Politics of Adoption and Reproduction." *Duke Journal of Gender Law and Policy* 2 (1995): 5–14.

——. "Race Separatism in the Family: More on the Transracial Adoption Debate." *Duke Journal of Gender Law and Policy* 2 (1995): 99–105.

——. *Family Bonds: Adoption and the Politics of Parenting*. New York: Houghton Mifflin, 1993.

——. "Where Do Black Children Belong? The Politics of Race Matching in Adoption." *University of Pennsylvania Law Review* 139 (1991): 1163–1256.

Belkin, Lisa. "Getting the Girl." *New York Times Magazine*, 25 July 1999, 26.

Benning, Victoria, and Philip Bennett. "Racial Lines Show New Generation." *Boston Globe*, 13 September 1992, 30–31.

Berry, Karin D. "Adoption, Race, and Red Tape." *Emerge*, April 1995, 40–46.

Black Male: Representations of Masculinity in Contemporary American Art. New York: Whitney Museum of Art, 1994.

Blight, David W., and Robert Gooding-Williams, eds. *The Souls of Black Folk*, by W. E. B. Du Bois. New York: Bedford Books, 1997.

Blum, Lawrence. "Multicultural Education as Values in Education." *Harvard Children's Initiative*. Cambridge, Mass., 1997.

Bolick, Clint. "Clinton's Quota Queens." *Wall Street Journal*, 30 April 1993, A12.

Bowen, James. "Cultural Convergences and Divergences: The Nexus between Putative Afro-American Family Values and the Best Interests of the Child." *Journal of Family Law* 26 (1987–1988): 487–544.

Bracey, John; August Meier; and Elliott Rudwick. *Black Nationalism in America*. New York: Bobbs-Merill, 1970.

Butler, Judith. *Bodies That Matter: On the Discursive Limits of "Sex"*. New York: Routledge, 1993.

Cardozo, Benjamin. *The Nature of the Judicial Process*. New Haven, Conn.: Yale University Press, 1921.

Carens, Joseph H. "Realistic and Idealistic Approaches to the Ethics of Migration." *International Migration Review* 30, no.1 (Spring 1996): 156–70.

Carroll, Rebecca, and Bill Dockery. "The Debate over Cross-Racial Adoption: An Odd Coalition Takes Aim at a Decades-Old Prejudice Against Transracial Placements." *USA Weekend Magazine*, 17–19 March 1995.

Carter, Stephen L. "Do Courts Matter?" 90 *Michigan Law Review* (1992): 1222–23.

Cohen, Cathy J. *The Boundaries of Blackness: AIDS and the Breakdown of Black Politics*. Chicago: University of Chicago Press, 1999.

Collins, Patricia Hill. *Fighting Back: Black Women and the Search for Justice*. Minneapolis: University of Minnesota Press, 1998.

Conley, Dalton. *Being Black, Living In the Red*. Berkeley: University of California Press, 1999.

Cornell, Drucilla. *Just Cause: Freedom, Identity, and Rights*. New York: Rowman & Littlefield, 2000.

Courtney, Mark. "The Politics and Realities of Transracial Adoption." *Child Welfare* 126 (November–December 1997): 749–79.

Crenshaw, Kimberle et. al., eds. *Critical Race Theory: The Key Writings That Formed the Movement*. New York: New Press, 1995.

——. "Race, Reform, and Reentrenchment: Transformation and Legitimation in Antidiscrimination Law." *Harvard Law Review* 101 (1988): 1331–87.

Cross, June. "Secret Daughter." *Radcliffe Quarterly* (Winter 1997): 26–28.

Crossen, Cynthia. "Hard Choices: In Today's Adoptions, the Biological Parents Are Calling the Shots." *Wall Street Journal*, 14 September 1989, 1.

Cruse, Harold. *The Crisis of the Negro Intellectual*. New York: William Morrow, 1967.

Dahl, Robert A. *Pluralist Democracy in the United States*. Chicago: Rand McNally, 1967.

Davis, F. James. *Who Is Black? One Nation's Definition*. University Park: Pennsylvania State University Press, 1991.

Dawson, Michael. *Behind the Mule: Race and Class in African-American Politics*. Princeton: Princeton University Press, 1994.

DeBerry, K. M., S. Scarr, and R. Weinberg. "Family Racial Socialization and Ecological Competence: Longitudinal Assessments of African-American Transracial Adoptees." *Child Development* 67 (1996): 2375–2399.

Derricotte, Toi. *The Black Notebooks: An Interior Journey*. New York: W. W. Norton, 1997.

Du Bois, W. E. B. *The Souls of Black Folk*. New York: Penguin Books, 1989.

Early, Gerald, ed. *Lure and Loathing: Essays on Race, Identity, and the Ambivalence of Assimilation*. New York: Penguin Press, 1993.

Elshtain, Jean Bethke. *Democracy on Trial*. New York: BasicBooks, 1995.

Ely, John Hart. *Democracy and Distrust: A Theory of Judical Review*. Cambridge, Mass.: Harvard University Press, 1980.

Essien-Udom, E. U. *Black Nationalism: A Search for an Identity in America*. Chicago: University of Chicago Press, 1962.

Etzioni, Amitai, ed. *The Essential Communitarian Reader*. New York: Rowman & Littlefield, 1998.

Fanon, Frantz. *Black Skin, White Masks*. New York: Grove Press, 1967.

———. *The Wretched of the Earth: The Handbook for the Black Revolution That Is Changing the World*. New York: Grove Press, 1963.

Fein, Esther B. "Secrecy and Stigma No Longer Clouding Adoptions." *New York Times*, 25 October 1998, 1.

Foucault, Michel. *The History of Sexuality*. Vol. 1. New York: Vintage Books, 1990.

———. *Madness and Civilization: A History of Insanity in the Age of Reason*. New York: Random House, 1965.

Fraser, Nancy and Linda Gordon. "A Genealogy of *Dependency*." 19 *Signs: Journal of Women in Culture and Society* (Winter 1994): 309–336.

Funderburg, Lise. *Black, White, Other: Biracial Americans Talk About Race and Identity*. New York: William Morrow, 1994.

Gaines, Kevin. "Race and Racism." *Social Text* 42 (1995) 45–52.

Gilroy, Paul. *The Black Atlantic: Modernity and Double-Consciousness*. Cambridge, Mass.: Harvard University Press, 1993.

Glendon, Mary Ann. *Rights Talk: The Impoverishment of Political Discourse*. New York: Free Press, 1991.

Goldstein, Joseph; Albert J. Solnit; Sonja Goldstein; and Anna Freud. *The*

Best Interests of the Child: The Least Detrimental Alternative. New York: Free Press, 1996.

Gooding-Williams, Robert. "Race, Multiculturalism, and Democracy." *Constellations: An International Journal of Critical and Democratic Theory* 5, no.1 (1998): 18–36.

——, ed. *Reading Rodney King/Reading Urban Uprising*. New York: Routledge, 1993.

Gould, Stephen Jay. *The Mismeasure of Man*. New York: Norton, 1981.

Griffin, John Howard. *Black like Me*. Boston: Houghton Mifflin, 1961.

Gutmann, Amy, ed. *Freedom of Association*. Princeton, N.J.: Princeton University Press, 1998.

Gutmann, Amy, and Dennis Thompson. *Democracy and Disagreement*. Cambridge, Mass.: Harvard University Press, 1996.

——, ed. *Multiculturalism*. Princeton, N.J.: Princeton University Press, 1994.

Guy-Sheftall, Beverly, ed. *Words of Fire: An Anthology of African-American Feminist Thought*. New York: New Press, 1995.

Hamilton, Charles, and Kwame Ture. *Black Power: The Politics of Liberation*. New York: Random House, 1967.

Harper, Phillip Brian. *Are We Not Men? Masculine Anxiety and the Problem of African-American Identity*. New York: Oxford University Press, 1996.

Haslanger, Sally and Charlotte Witt, eds. *The View From Home: Philosophical and Feminist Issues in Adoption*. Boulder, Col.: Westview Press, 2002.

Herrnstein, Richard, and Charles Murray. *The Bell Curve: Intelligence and Class Structure in American Life*. New York: Free Press, 1994.

Higginbotham, Evelyn Brooks. "African-American Women's History and the Metalanguage of Race." *Signs: Journal of Women in Culture and Society*. 17 (Winter 1992): 251–74.

Holmes, Stephen. "Bitter Racial Dispute Rages over Adoption." *New York Times*, 13 April 1995, A16.

hooks, bell. *Black Looks: Race and Representation*. Boston: South End Press, 1992.

Horwitz, Morton. *The Transformation of American Law, 1870–1960: The Crisis of Legal Orthodoxy*. New York: Oxford University Press, 1992.

Howard, Margaret. "Transracial Adoption: An Analysis of the Best Interests Standard." *Notre Dame Law Review* 59 (1984): 503–55.

Howe, Ruth-Arlene. "Transracial Adoption (TRA): Old Prejudices and Discrimination Float under a New Halo." *Boston University Public Interest Law Journal* 6 (Winter 1997): 409–72.

——. "Redefining the Transracial Adoption Controversy." *Duke Journal of Gender Law and Policy* 2 (Spring 1995): 131–64.

——. "Adoption Practice, Issues and Laws, 1958–1983." *Family Law Quarterly* 17 (1983): 173–97.

Hull, Gloria T., Patricia Bell Scott, and Barbara Smith. *All The Women Are White, All The Blacks Are Men, But Some of Us Are Brave*. Old Westbury, NY: Feminist Press, 1982.

Hunter, James Davison, and Os Guiness, eds. *Articles of Faith, Articles of Peace*. Washington, DC: Brookings Institution, 1990.

Institute for Justice. "Opposition Motion." *Boston University Public Interest Law Journal* 6 (Winter 1997): 473–525.

Johnson, Dirk. "Former Cocaine User Regains Child in Custody Case." *New York Times*, 9 March 1999.

Johnston, Patricia Irwin. *Adopting after Fertility*. Indianapolis: Perspectives Press, 1996.

Kateb, George. "Response to Robert Gooding-Williams." *Constellations: An International Journal of Critical and Democratic Theory* 5, no. 1 (1998): 48–50.

Katz, Stanley N. "The Strange Birth and Unlikely History of Constitutional Equality." *Journal of American History* 75, no. 3 (December 1988): 747–62.

Kennedy, Randall. "Orphans of Separatism: The Painful Politics of Transracial Adoption." *American Prospect* (Spring 1995): 38–45.

——. *Race, Crime, and the Law*. New York: Vintage, 1997.

Kovel, Joel. *White Racism: A Psychohistory*. New York: Vintage Books, 1970.

Kymlicka, Will. *Liberalism, Community, and Culture*. New York: Oxford University Press, 1989.

——, ed. *The Rights of Minority Cultures*. New York: Oxford University Press, 1995.

Ladner, Joyce. *Mixed Families: Adopting across Racial Boundaries*. New York: Archer Press, Doubleday, 1977.

Landes, Elisabeth, and Richard Posner. "The Economics of the Baby Shortage." *Journal of Legal Studies* 7 (1978): 323–48.

Larsen, Nella. *Quicksand and Passing*. New Brunswick, N.J.: Rutgers University Press, 1986. Edited by Deborah McDowell.

Lawrence, Charles III. "The Id, the Ego, and Equal Protection: Reckoning with Unconscious Racism." *Stanford Law Review* 39 (1987): 317–88.

Lehmann-Haupt, Christopher. "A Multiculturalist with Regrets." *New York Times*, 20 March 1997, C18.

Lorde, Audre. *Sister Outsider: Essays and Speeches*. Trumansburg, NY: Crossing Press, 1984.

Loury, Glenn C. *One by One from the Inside Out: Essays and Interviews on Race and Responsibility in America*. New York: Free Press, 1995.

McBride, James. *The Color of Water: A Black Man's Tribute to His White Mother*. New York: Riverhead Books, 1996.

McLarin, Kim. "Primary Colors: The Mother Is Black; Her Interracial Daughter Is Fair-Skinned. Society Has Trouble Seeing Their Connection." *New York Times Magazine*, 24 May 1998, 58.

Marriot, Michael. "Frank Racial Dialogue Thrives on the Web." *New York Times*, 8 March 1998, 1.

Massey, Douglas S., and Nancy A. Denton. *American Apartheid: Segregation and the Making of the Underclass*. Cambridge: Harvard University Press, 1993.

Mead, Lawrence. *Beyond Entitlement: The Social Obligations of Citizenship*. New York: Free Press, 1986.

Merritt, William T. Excerpt from testimony by William T. Merritt, president of the National Association of Black Social Workers, during U.S. Senate Hearings of the Committee on Labor and Human Resources, 25 June 1985.

Mills, Charles W. *The Racial Contract*. Ithaca, N.Y.: Cornell University Press, 1997.

Minow, Martha. *Not Only for Myself: Identity, Politics & the Law*. New York: New Press, 1997.

Morrison, Toni. *Playing in the Dark: Whiteness and the Literary Imagination*. Cambridge, Mass.: Harvard University Press, 1992.

Mosher, Stephen W. "The Repackaging of Margaret Sanger." *Wall Street Journal*. 5 May 1997, A18.

Murray, Charles. *Losing Ground: American Social Policy, 1950–1980*. New York: Basic Books, 1984.

National Association of Black Social Workers. "Position Statement: "Preserving African American Families." Detroit: National Association of Black Social Workers, 1994.

Neufeld, John. *Edgar Allen*. New York: Signet Press, 1968.

Nussbaum, Martha, ed. *For Love of Country: Debating the Limits of Patriotism*. Boston: Beacon Press, 1996.

Okin, Susan Moller. *Justice, Gender, and the Family*. New York: Basic Books, 1989.

Omi, Michael, and Howard Winant. *Racial Formation in the United States: From the 1960s to the 1990s*. New York: Routledge, 1994.

Packer, Z. Z. "Drinking Coffee Elsewhere." *New Yorker*, 19–26 June 2000: 156–70.

Pateman, Carol. *The Sexual Contract*. Stanford, Calif.: Stanford University Press, 1988.

Patterson, Orlando. *The Ordeal of Integration: Progress and Resentment in America's "Racial" Crisis*. Washington, D.C.: Civitas, 1997.

——. *Slavery and Social Death*. Cambridge, Mass.: Harvard University Press, 1982.

Perry, Twila. "The Transracial Adoption Controversy: An Analysis of Discourse and Subordination." *New York University Review of Law and Social Change* 21 (1993–1994): 33–108.

——. "Race and Child Placement: The Best Interests Test and the Cost of Discretion." *Journal of Family Law* 29 (1990–1991): 51–127.

Posner, Richard. *Sex and Reason*. Cambridge, Mass.: Harvard University Press, 1992.

Purdum, Todd S. "California Census Confirms Whites Are in Minority." *New York Times*, 30 March 2001, A1.

Radin, Margaret Jane. "Market Inalienability," 100 *Harvard Law Review* 1849 (June 1987): 1849–1937.

Rawls, John. *A Theory of Justice*. Cambridge, Mass.: Harvard University Press, 1971.

Reddy, Maureen T. *Crossing the Color Line: Race, Parenting, and Culture*. New Brunswick, N.J.: Rutgers University Press, 1994.

Reed Jr., Adolph. "The Underclass as Myth and Symbol." *Radical America* 24 (January 1992): 21–40.

——. ed. *Without Justice For All: The New Liberalism and Our Retreat From Racial Equality*. Boulder, Col.: Westview Press, 1999.

Roberts, Dorothy E. *Killing the Black Body: Race, Reproduction, and the Meaning of Liberty*. New York: Random House, 1997.

Roediger, David R. *The Wages of Whiteness: Race and the Making of the American Working Class*. New York: Verso, 1991.

Rogin, Michael and Robert Post, eds. *Race and Representation: Affirmative Action*. New York: Zone Books, 1998.

Rorty, Amélie O., ed. *Explaining Emotions*. Berkeley: University of California Press, 1980.

Rorty, Richard. *Contingency, Irony, and Solidarity*. New York: Cambridge University Press, 1989.

Rose, Tricia. *Black Noise: Rap Music and Culture in Contemporary Black America*. Wesleyan, Mass.: Wesleyan University Press, 1994.

Rosenberg, Gerald N. *The Hollow Hope: Can Courts Bring About Social Change?* Chicago: University of Chicago Press, 1991.

Rush, Sharon. *Loving Across the Color Line: A White Adoptive Mother Learns About Race*. Lanham, MD: Rowman and Littlefield, 2000.

Sandel, Michael. *Democracy's Discontent: America in Search of a Public Philosophy*. Cambridge, Mass.: Harvard University Press, 1996.

——, ed. *Liberalism and Its Critics*. New York: New York University Press, 1984.

——. *Liberalism and the Limits of Justice*. New York: Cambridge University Press, 1982.

Sartre, Jean-Paul. *Black Orpheus*. Translated by S. W. Allen. Paris: Editions Giallimard, 1963.

——. *Existentialism and Human Emotions*. Translated by Bernard Frechtman and Hazel E. Barnes. New York: Wisdom Library: distributed by Citadel Press, 1957.

——. *Being and Nothingness: An Essay on Phenomenological Ontology*. Translated by Hazel E. Barnes. New York: Philosophical Library, 1956.

——. *Anti-Semite and Jew*. Translated by George J. Becker. New York: Schocken Books, 1948.

Scales-Trent, Judy. *Notes of a White Black Woman*. University Park: Pennsylvania State University Press, 1995.

Schattschneider, E. E. *The Semisovereign People: A Realist's View of Democracy in America*. New York: Holt, Rinehart and Winston, 1960.

Schulman, S., and W. Darity, eds. *The Question of Discrimination: Racial Inequality in the U.S. Labor Market*. Middletown, Conn.: Wesleyan University Press, 1989.

Scott, Janny, "Races Still Live Apart in New York." *New York Times*, 23 March 2001, B1.

Shanley, Mary Lyndon. *Making Babies, Making Families: What Matters Most in an Age of Reproductive Technologies, Surrogacy, Adoption, and Same-Sex and Unwed Parents*. Boston: Beacon Press, 2001.

Simon, Rita J.; Howard Altstein; and Marygold S. Melli. *The Case for Transracial Adoption*. Washington, D.C.: American University Press, 1994.

Simon, Rita J. and Rhonda M. Roorda. *In Their Own Voices: Transracial Adoptees Tell Their Stories*. New York: Columbia University Press, 2000.

Skolnick, Arlene. *Embattled Paradise: The American Family in an Age of Uncertainty*. New York: Basic Books, 1991.

Smolowe, Jill. "Adoption in Black and White." *Time*, 14 August 1995, 50.

Sowell, Thomas. *Civil Rights: Rhetoric or Reality?* New York: William Morrow, 1984.

Stack, Carol. *All Our Kin: Strategies For Survival In a Black Community*. New York: Harper and Row, 1974.

Steele, Shelby. *A Dream Deferred: The Second Betrayal of Black Freedom in America*. New York: HarperPerennial Library, 1999.

——. *The Content of Our Character: A New Vision of Race in America*. New York: HarperCollins, 1990.

Strolovitch, Dara Z. *Closer to a Pluralist Heaven? Advocacy Groups, and the Politics of Representation*. Ph.D. Diss. New Haven, Conn.: Yale University Press, 2002.

Takaki, Ronald. *A Different Mirror: A History of Multicultural America*. Boston: Little, Brown, 1993.

Tate, Katherine. *From Protest to Politics: The New Black Voters in American Elections*. New York: Russell Sage Foundation, 1993.

Thornton, Russell. "What the Census Doesn't Count." *New York Times*, 23 March 2001, A19.

Ture, Kwame, (formerly known as Stokely Carmichael) and Charles V. Hamilton. *Black Power: The Politics of Liberation*. New York: Random House, 1967.

Wadia-Ells, Susan, ed. *The Adoption Reader*. Seattle: Seal Press, 1995.

Waldron, Jan. *Giving Away Simone*. New York: Random House, 1995.

Waldron, Jeremy. "What is Cosmopolitan?" *Journal of Political Philosophy*. 8 (2000): 227–43.

Walzer, Michael. *What It Means to Be an American: Essays on the American Experience*. New York: Marsilio Publishers, 1996.

——. *Spheres of Justice: A Defense of Pluralism and Equality*. New York: Basic Books, 1983.

Waters, Mary C. *Ethnic Options: Choosing Identities in America*. Berkeley: University of California Press, 1990.

Weisberg, Jacob. "For the Sake of Argument." *New York Times Magazine*, 5 November 2000, 48.

West, Robin. "Universalism, Liberal Theory, and the Problem of Gay Marriage." 25 *Florida State University Law Review* (Summer 1998): 705–30.

Williams, Lena. "*Losing Isaiah*: Truth in Shades of Gray." *New York Times*, 23 March 1995, C1.

Williams, Patricia J. *Seeing a Color-blind Future: The Paradox of Race (The 1997 BBC Reith Lectures)*. New York: Noonday Press, 1997.

——. *The Rooster's Egg: On the Persistence of Prejudice*. Cambridge, Mass.: Harvard University Press, 1995.

Wilogoren, Jodi. "U.S. Court Bars Race as Factor In School Entry." *New York Times*. 28 March 2001, A1.

Wing, Adrienne, ed. *Critical Race Feminism*. New York: Routledge, 1997.

Wright, Lawrence. "One Drop of Blood." *New Yorker*, 25 July 1994, 46–55.

Young, Iris Marion. *Justice and the Politics of Difference*. Princeton, N.J.: Princeton University Press, 1990.

Zack, Naomi. *Race and Mixed Race*. Philadelphia: Temple University Press, 1993.

Cases

Index